Lab Manual to Accompany

Pascal: A Guided Tour

Turbo Pascal Version

Leland L. Beck

San Diego State University

C_EP

Computer Education Press

San Diego

The cover design and portions of the Pascal programs in this manual are reproduced from *Pascal: A Guided Tour* by Leland L. Beck, © 1994 by Addison-Wesley Publishing Company, Inc. Reprinted by permission of the publisher.

Many of the designations used by manufacturers and sellers to distinguish their products are claimed as trademarks. Where those designations appear in this book, and the publisher was aware of a trademark claim, the designations have been printed in caps or initial caps.

The programs, applications, and instructions presented in this book have been included for their educational value. They have been tested with care, but are not guaranteed for any particular purpose. The publisher does not offer any warranties or representations, nor does it accept any liabilities with respect to the programs, applications, and instructions.

ISBN 1-884808-02-6

 **PREFACE**

The textbook *Pascal: A Guided Tour* is designed around a set of realistic, yet understandable, example programs. There are programs for codebreaking, finding anagrams, simulating a simple ecological system, and a variety of other applications. Students learn how to program by first reading, modifying, and experimenting with these example programs. This approach to teaching programming relies on a laboratory experience that is closely integrated with the text.

This lab manual is designed to support and enhance such a laboratory experience. There are many new things to be learned as the student begins to study programming. Our goal is to make learning these things as easy as possible.

The instructions and discussions in this lab manual are closely tied to the exercises in *Pascal: A Guided Tour*. In the beginning, every exercise that involves using the computer is described in detail. Keystroke-level instructions show the student how to edit, compile and execute programs, and how to use other features of Turbo Pascal. As the student becomes more familiar with how to perform these operations, the instructions become less detailed. Discussions in later chapters focus on the new concepts that are being learned, and on implementation-dependent details of the Pascal language.

Special "quick reference" sections of this manual summarize the most commonly used DOS and Turbo Pascal commands. Complete listings of the example programs from the first eight chapters of *Pascal: A Guided Tour* are included for ease of reference. There are also listings of source code files that are used throughout the text to provide support for abstract data types and for operations such as cursor positioning and random number generation.

This lab manual is designed for use with Version 7.0 of Turbo Pascal; instructions for use with Version 6.0 are also included. Other versions of the lab manual are available for UNIX and other commonly used hardware/software environments. For more information, or to make comments or suggestions about the manual, contact the author at San Diego State University (e-mail: beck@cs.sdsu.edu).

The author is grateful to Addison-Wesley Publishing Company for permission to use the example programs and the cover design.

L. L. B.
San Diego, California

 **CONTENTS**

Guide to the Exercises

Example Programs

CHAPTER

1

Introduction

The exercises you are about to do will show you how to run some of the example programs from this book on your computer. The computer you are using for this course is called a PC (personal computer). The term *personal computer* originally referred to any computer that is normally used by only one person at a time. However, today the term PC usually refers to an IBM PC or a similar computer made by some other manufacturer.

The computer that you will use runs under the control of a special kind of program called an *operating system.* When you type commands and programs at the keyboard, you are actually communicating with this operating system. It keeps track of your programs, and operates the computer itself to do the things that you request.

The operating system used on your computer is named DOS. There are several different versions of DOS. However, most of the commands you will need to do the exercises in this book are the same, regardless of which version of DOS you are using. Your instructor will tell you if there are any differences you need to know about.

Getting Started

Before you can start using the computer, it must be turned on and DOS must be ready to accept your commands. DOS tells you that it is ready by displaying a *prompt* at the beginning of a line on the screen. This prompt starts with a letter (usually A, B, or C), and ends with >. There may be some other symbols between the letter and the >. For example, the following are all valid DOS prompts:

```
C:\>

A:\>

B:\CHAP2>

C:\PROGRAMS\CHAP1>
```

If there is no prompt on your screen, but the computer appears to be turned on, try pressing the key marked <Enter> or <Return> to see if a prompt appears.

If a DOS prompt like those just described appears on your screen, you are ready to start using the computer. If there is no prompt, you will need to restart DOS. This process is called *booting the system.* The exact method for doing this depends on how your laboratory is set up -- your instructor will tell you how to proceed. At the end of the booting process, DOS will display a prompt to tell you that it is ready to accept your commands.

Using Your Program Disk

Programs and data used by a computer are usually stored on a disk. Your instructor will tell you how to get a disk that contains the programs from the first few chapters of this book. (This kind of disk is often called a *diskette* or a *floppy disk,* to distinguish it from the *hard disk* that is permanently attached to the computer.)

The computer you are using has one or more diskette drives that will fit your program disk. (Some computers have two different kinds of diskette drives, to fit different types of disks.) Each drive is identified by a letter of the alphabet. If your computer has only one diskette drive, it is drive A. If there are two drives, the upper (or left-hand) drive is usually drive A and the other is usually drive B. Insert your program disk into drive A. Depending on the type of diskette you are using, you may also need to close an access door on the drive.

Now type the command

```
a:
```

and press <Enter>. (On some keyboards, this key may be marked <Return> or ↵ instead of <Enter>.) This tells DOS that you want to begin using files from the disk in drive A. If you accidentally put your disk in the wrong drive (or if you typed the command a: before inserting your disk in the drive), you will get an error message that looks like

```
Not ready error reading drive A
Abort, Retry, Fail?
```

If this happens to you, type f (for Fail); you should then see the message

```
Current drive is no longer valid>
```

This is a normal part of recovering from the original error. Now insert your disk in drive A and type the command a: again.

After you enter the command a: your prompt should change to something that looks like

```
A:\>
```

In some cases, you may find that there are other characters in the prompt between the
`A:` and the `>`. For example, your prompt might look like

        `A:\CHAP2>`

If this happens, type the command

        `cd \`

and press <Enter>; you should then get the correct prompt as shown above. (The `\`
is a "backslash" character that is not found on most ordinary typewriter keyboards --
be careful not to confuse it with the "forward slash" character `/`.)

As you do the exercises in Chapter 1 of your text, you will be using the programs
from your disk. After you have finished using the computer, remember to remove
your program disk and take it with you. You will use this disk, and others that you
will create, throughout the course.

Exercise 1.1

Now you are ready to begin using the computer to run programs. Several example
programs are already stored on your program disk for you to use. To see a list of
these, type the command

        `dir`

following the DOS prompt, and then press <Enter>. You should see a listing that
looks like the following:

        `Directory of A:\`

ANAGRAM	PAS	53297	3-09-94	11:48a
COUNT		14	3-17-94	2:36p
CRYPTO		5081	3-09-94	11:48a
LOAN	PAS	7300	3-09-94	11:48a
SOLVE	PAS	49429	3-09-94	11:48a
WATOR	PAS	77538	3-15-94	11:15a
CHAP2	<DIR>		3-17-94	1:49p
CHAP3	<DIR>		3-17-94	1:49p

This is a listing of the *directory* of your disk. It shows the names of all the files on
the disk, and other information about the files and about the disk itself. The listing
you get may be arranged differently, and the dates and times may be different.
However, it should contain the same file names.

The example program you will run in this exercise is named Loan. It is stored in a
file named `LOAN.PAS`. Under DOS, the name of a file can include an *extension* that
describes the kind of information stored in the file. In this case, the extension `.PAS`

indicates that the file contains a Pascal program. Notice that the extension is listed in the directory in a separate column, without the period. Some files in this directory, such as COUNT and CRYPTO, do not have extensions.

In this course, you will use a system called Turbo Pascal to write and run Pascal programs. Type the command

```
turbo loan.pas
```

following the DOS prompt, and then press <Enter>. When you are using DOS, commands and file names can be typed using either uppercase or lowercase letters. It does not matter whether you type a file name as loan.pas, LOAN.PAS, or Loan.Pas -- all of these refer to the same file. Likewise, you could type the first part of the command as turbo or TURBO. In this manual, we will always show DOS commands using lowercase letters.

After a few seconds, the display on your screen will change to look like this:

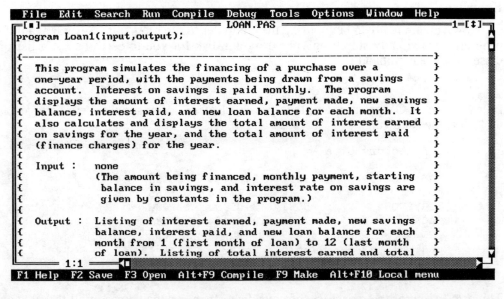

This is the first part of the Pascal program Loan. In Chapter 2, you will begin to study this program in detail. For now, however, all we want to do is run the program to see how it works.

When you are using Turbo Pascal, you can select what you want to do from a series of *menus*. The line at the top of the screen shows the menus that are available for you to use -- these menus are named File, Edit, Search, etc. You can access the menus by using special *function keys* on your keyboard. These keys are labeled <F1> through <F10>; you will probably find them along the top of your keyboard or at the left-hand side. There are also four *arrow keys* that are labeled ↑, ←, →, and ↓. These are probably on the right-hand side of your keyboard.

To activate the menus, press the key marked <F10>. Notice that the name of the File menu in the menu bar is now highlighted. You can change the menu that is highlighted by using the keys ← and →. Press → until the name of the Compile menu is highlighted. Now press <Enter> to activate the Compile menu. Your display should now look like this:

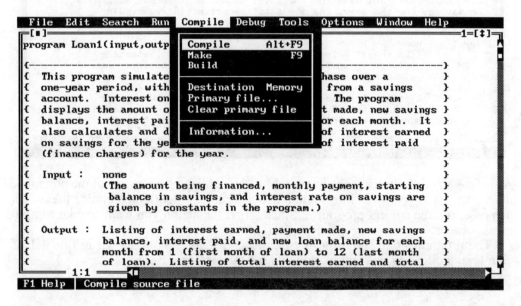

The Compile menu contains several items to choose from. The first of these items (also named Compile) is highlighted. In this exercise, you want to compile the program (that is, translate it from Pascal into machine language) so the computer can run it. Since the action you want to take is already highlighted, simply press <Enter>. You will see a box on the screen that displays some information about the compilation, and then the message

```
Compile successful: Press any key
```

Press <Enter> and the box will disappear.

Now that you have successfully compiled the program, the next step is to run it. Press <F10> again to activate the menu bar. Use the arrow keys ← and → to highlight the name of the Run menu, and press <Enter> to activate this menu.

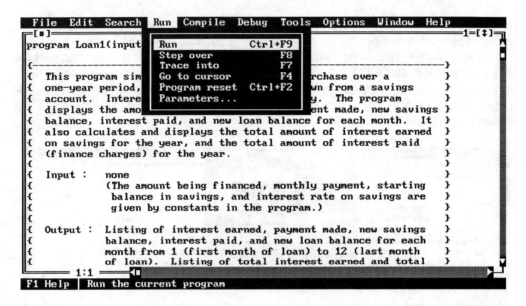

As before, the first choice in the menu is already highlighted. The line at the bottom of the screen gives you more information about what this highlighted choice means (in this case, run the current program). Since this is the action you want to take, simply press <Enter>.

The program Loan should now run, displaying the output shown in Fig. 1.1 of your text. Following this output, you will see the message

```
    Press return to exit program
```

This message is the last thing displayed by the program Loan. When you press <Enter>, you will return to the original Turbo Pascal screen with the menus.

This completes Exercise 1.1. You can exit from Turbo Pascal and return to DOS by using the File menu. Follow the same steps that you have used before. First press <F10> to activate the menu bar; then use the arrow keys to highlight the name of the File menu and press <Enter> to activate it.

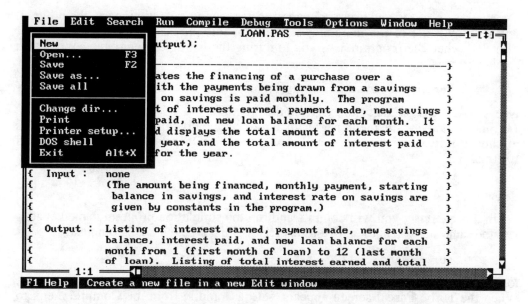

This time, the action you want to take is not the one that is already highlighted. Use the ↓ key to move the highlighting down to the last item on the list (Exit). Notice that the line at the bottom of the screen now describes what you want to do (Exit Turbo Pascal). Now press <Enter> to perform this action. The program and menus will disappear, and you will see a DOS prompt appear again at the bottom of your screen.

Exercise 1.3

This exercise asks you to run the program named Anagram. To do this, you will use the same steps that you did for Loan. At the DOS prompt, type

```
turbo anagram.pas
```

and press <Enter>. When the Turbo Pascal screen appears, activate the menu bar by pressing <F10>. Highlight the name of the Compile menu and press <Enter> to activate this menu. Select the highlighted choice (Compile) from this menu by pressing <Enter> again. After the compilation is complete, press <Enter> to return to the original screen. (If you make a mistake and activate the wrong menu at any time, you can cancel the action by pressing the key marked <Esc> or <Escape>.)

Next activate the menu bar again (by pressing <F10>), and select the Run menu (by highlighting its name and pressing <Enter>). Press <Enter> again to choose Run from this menu and begin running the program Anagram. The program will ask you for a target word by displaying the message

```
Enter target word(s):
```

Type my computer and press <Enter>. After scanning its dictionary, the program will display a list of the anagrams it finds for this phrase. Press <Return> (or <Enter>) when the program asks you to during the listing of anagrams. When you receive the message

```
Another target word? (y/n) :
```

type n and press <Enter> to exit from the program.

Finally, activate the menu bar again and select the File menu. Use the arrow keys to choose Exit from this menu and return to the DOS prompt, just as you did in Exercise 1.1.

Exercise 1.4

In this exercise, you will compile and run the simulation program named Wator. Use the same steps as in the previous exercises. First type the DOS command

```
turbo wator.pas
```

to start Turbo Pascal. Remember to press <Enter> after you type this command. When the Turbo Pascal screen appears, select Compile from the Compile menu to translate the program into machine language. Then select Run from the Run menu to begin running the program. Remember that you can always cancel a mistake that you make with the menus by pressing <Esc>.

When the program asks for parameter values, simply press <Enter> for each parameter. (As described in the text, this accepts the default values for the parameters.) After the parameter selection is complete, you will see the simulation displayed on your computer screen. When you get the message

```
Continue? (y/n) :
```

type either y or n and press <Enter>. At the end of the simulation, you will press <Enter> to exit from the program and return to the Turbo Pascal screen.

If you want to run the program again, you can do so by simply selecting Run from the Run menu. It is not necessary to compile the program again. Finally, select Exit from the File menu to leave Turbo Pascal.

Exercise 1.5

Follow the same steps as in previous exercises to compile and run the program Solve. This program displays an encoded message on the screen, and then helps you try letter substitutions in an attempt to solve the puzzle. To become familiar with how the program works, enter the sequence of commands described on pp. 13-17 in your text. After the program has finished, you can run it with a different cryptogram by selecting Run from the Run menu again.

Menu Shortcuts (optional)

The methods you have learned in this chapter can be used with all of the Turbo Pascal menus. However, there are several shortcuts that can make using the menus easier. Notice that the first letter of the name of each menu in the menu bar is highlighted in a different color from the rest. You can activate a menu directly by holding down the key marked <Alt> and typing the highlighted letter of the menu name. For example, you could activate the File menu by typing <Alt+F> or the Compile menu by typing <Alt+C>, instead of using <F10> and the arrow keys.

Similarly, each item in a menu has a highlighted letter. For example, when the Compile menu is active you will notice that the first letter of the "Compile" item is highlighted. You can select this item by simply typing the highlighted letter. (It is not necessary to use the <Alt> key when selecting items from a menu.) Likewise, you can select Exit from the File menu by simply typing the highlighted letter, instead of using the arrow keys. (In this case, you will notice that the highlighted letter of Exit is the "x", not the "E".)

It is even possible to select some items without activating menus at all. For example, look again at the File menu.

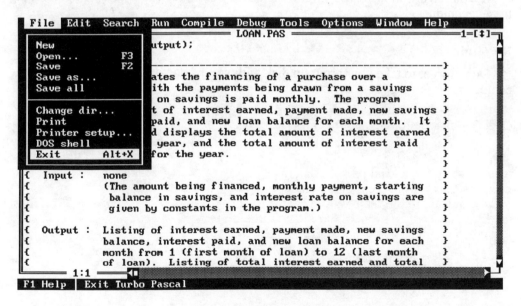

Notice the "Alt+X" that appears beside the Exit item in this menu. You can select Exit directly at any time (without needing to activate the File menu) by simply typing <Alt+X>. (In Turbo Pascal, the <Alt+X> is referred to as a *hot key* because you can use it at any time.) Similarly, you can select Compile from the Compile menu at any time by using the hot key <Alt+F9>. (See the Compile menu shown in the discussion of Exercise 1.1.) The bottom line of the screen will help remind you of some of these hot keys. For example, the bottom line of the main Turbo Pascal screen shows that <Alt+F9> is a hot key for Compile.

If you are interested, you might want to try some of the exercises again, using these shortcuts.

Using a Mouse (optional)

If your computer is equipped with a mouse, you can also use it to select items from menus. As you move the mouse on the mouse pad, you will notice that a pointer moves on the screen. You can activate a menu by moving the pointer to the name of that menu and clicking the mouse button. (If your mouse has more than one button, the leftmost one is probably the correct one to use.) You can select an item from an active menu by moving the pointer to that item and clicking the button again. It is also possible to combine these two operations. You can move the pointer to the name of a menu and then press the mouse button and hold it down. Then you can select an item by moving to that item before you release the button. (Moving the mouse in this way, while holding the button down, is called *dragging* the mouse.)

If you have a mouse, you might want to try some of the exercises again using these techniques.

Reminder

Don't forget to take your program disk with you when you have finished using the computer!

CHAPTER

2

In Chapter 1, you compiled and ran programs that already existed. As you do the exercises in this chapter, you will learn how to create new programs that do different things.

Begin by following the same "getting started" procedure as in Chapter 1. (If you have difficulty at any point, you may want to go back and reread the instructions for these steps from Chapter 1.) If the computer is turned off, or if you cannot get the DOS prompt, you may need to boot the system. Then insert your program disk into drive A and enter the commands

```
a:
cd \
```

so that your DOS prompt looks like

```
A:\>
```

Remember to wait for the prompt before typing a command, and remember to press <Enter> after each command. (This applies to all of the DOS commands that you will use. From now on, we will not repeat this reminder each time.)

Directories

Under DOS, files are stored in *directories*. In Chapter 1, you listed the names of the files on your program disk by entering the command

```
dir
```

If you do this now, you should see a listing that looks like

```
        Directory of A:\

ANAGRAM   PAS     53297    3-09-94    11:48a
COUNT               14     3-17-94     2:36p
CRYPTO            5081     3-09-94    11:48a
LOAN      PAS     7300     3-09-94    11:48a
SOLVE     PAS    49429     3-09-94    11:48a
WATOR     PAS    77538     3-15-94    11:15a
```

```
CHAP2      <DIR>        3-17-94    1:49p
CHAP3      <DIR>        3-17-94    1:49p
```

(As before, the file names may be arranged in a different order, and the dates and times may be different.) The files with names ending in .PAS are the Pascal programs that you ran in Chapter 1. CRYPTO and CCOUNT are data files used by these programs. For example, CRYPTO contains the cryptograms that are used by the program Solve.

The files named CHAP2 and CHAP3 are not ordinary files at all -- they are other directories. The directory CHAP2 contains all of the files you will need to do the exercises from Chapter 2 of your text. You can change to using this directory by entering the command

```
cd chap2
```

(As before, you can type commands and file names using either uppercase or lowercase letters.) When you have done this, your DOS prompt will change to look like

```
A:\CHAP2>
```

This reminds you that you are now in the directory CHAP2 on the disk in drive A. Now you can list the names of the files in this directory with the command

```
dir
```

If you do this now, you should see a listing like

```
Directory of A:\CHAP2

C2E11     PAS      7299     3-09-94    11:49a
C2E12     PAS      7269     3-09-94    11:49a
C2E13     PAS      7509     3-09-94    11:49a
C2E14     PAS      7300     3-09-94    11:49a
C2E15     PAS      7263     3-09-94    11:49a
C2E16     PAS      7254     3-09-94    11:49a
C2E17     PAS      7493     3-09-94    11:49a
LOAN1     PAS      7300     3-09-94    11:49a
LOANQTR   PAS      8504     3-09-94    11:49a
LOANVAR   PAS      8176     3-09-94    11:49a
```

There may also be directory entries with names like "." and ".." . These entries are used by DOS -- you do not need to be concerned with them.

You can change back to the main directory on your program disk by entering the command

```
cd \
```

as you did before. If you do another dir now, you will see the original listing of the main directory of your disk.

Exercise 2.1

If you entered the command `cd` as described at the end of the preceding section, you are back in the main directory of your program disk. Change to the directory CHAP2 and list the contents of this directory by entering the commands

```
cd chap2
dir
```

You will see the same listing of the directory CHAP2 as before.

Exercise 2.1 asks you to change the program Loan1 to create a new program named C2E1. The first step is to make a copy of Loan1. (We don't want to change Loan1 itself, because we will need to use it again later.) To do this, enter the command

```
copy loan1.pas c2e1.pas
```

(Remember that the names of files containing Pascal programs always end in .PAS.) This command copies the contents of LOAN1.PAS to a new file named C2E1.PAS. You can see the result of this by entering another `dir` command. If you do this now, you will see that a new file C2E1.PAS was created. Notice also that LOAN1.PAS is still present.

Exercise 2.1 asks you to make a change in C2E1.PAS, as described in your text. Start Turbo Pascal, as you did in Chapter 1, by entering the command

```
turbo c2e1.pas
```

You will see a screen that looks like this:

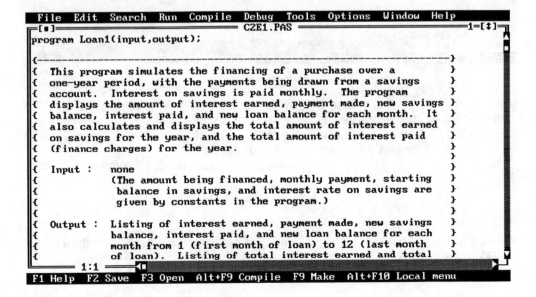

This is the first part of the program Loan1. Notice the *cursor* that is positioned at the beginning of the first line. In this manual, we will represent the cursor by ☐; on your screen, it will probably be an underline. It may be flashing to help you see it.

Exercise 2.1 asks us to change the `for` statement in the main program (see Fig. 2.2 in your text). The first thing we need to do is to find that statement in the program. Look for the keys on your keyboard labeled <PgDn> ("page down") and <PgUp> ("page up"). Press the key marked <PgDn> and you will see the display change to show the next "page" of the program. Press <PgDn> seven more times, and you will find the page that contains the `for` statement, as shown here:

```
  File   Edit   Search   Run   Compile   Debug   Tools   Options   Window   Help
┌─[■]════════════════════════════ C2E1.PAS ═══════════════════════════1=[↕]═┐
│ begin  { CleanUp }                                                        ▲│
│                                                                           ║│
│    write('Press return to exit program');                                ║│
│    readln                                                                  │
│                                                                            │
│  end;  { CleanUp }                                                         │
│                                                                            │
│{*****************************************************************}         │
│                                                                            │
│begin  { main program }                                                     │
│                                                                            │
│  { initialize variables and write headings }                              │
│                                                                            │
│  Initialize;                                                               │
│  WriteHeadings;                                                            │
│                                                                            │
│  { compute and write balances for each month of the loan }               ▓│
│                                                                            │
│  for Month := 1 to 12 do                                                   │
│    begin                                                                   │
│      ComputeNewBalance;                                                    ▼│
│═══ 161:1 ═══◄█────────────────────────────────────────────────────────►   │
  F1 Help  F2 Save  F3 Open  Alt+F9 Compile  F9 Make  Alt+F10 Local menu
```

If you accidentally go too far, use <PgUp> to move back up until you see the `for` statement on your screen. You are now looking at part of the main program from Loan1, which is shown in Fig. 2.2 of your text. Notice that the line numbers that appear in Fig. 2.2 are not actually a part of the program -- they were included in the text to make it easier to refer to different parts of the program.

Next use the ↓ key to move the cursor to the line we want to change, as shown here:

        ☐ for Month := 1 to 12 do

We want to change the `12` on this line to `6`. Use the → key to move right until the cursor is in this position:

```
for Month := 1 to 12 do
```

Now press the key marked <Del> to delete the character under the cursor. (On some keyboards, this key may be marked <Delete> or <Rubout>.) That leaves the line looking like

```
for Month := 1 to 2 do
```

Press the <Del> key again, and the line will be

```
for Month := 1 to  do
```

We have removed the 12 from the line; now all we have to do is insert the 6. You can insert text where the cursor is positioned by simply typing the characters you want to insert. If you now type 6 your line will look like

```
for Month := 1 to 6 do
```

This completes the changes we wanted to make in Loan1. Now you are ready to compile and run your new program. You can do this using the same menus you learned about in Chapter 1. First select Compile from the Compile menu to translate the program into machine language. Then select Run from the Run menu to execute the program. The results should be the same as those shown in Fig. 2.3 of your text.

As you made changes to the program in this exercise, you saw those changes appear on the screen. However, the changes are not yet reflected in the program file stored on your disk. Before leaving Turbo Pascal, you should save the new version of the program on your disk, so it is available in case you want to use it again. To do this, you can either select Save from the File menu or use the hot key <F2>. (Notice that the line at the bottom of the screen reminds you about this hot key.) Now you can leave Turbo Pascal by selecting Exit from the File menu, as before.

If you list the files in the directory CHAP2 now (using the dir command), you will see a new file named C2E1.BAK. This file contains the previous version of C2E1 (the one before you made the changes in this exercise). The extension .BAK stands for "backup". Whenever you change a file using Turbo Pascal, the previous version is automatically saved in this way. However, only one previous version of each file is kept. Thus if you change a file twice, only the current version and the latest back-up version are available.

Exercise 2.2

This exercise asks you to make another change in Loan1, creating a new program named C2E2. As in Exercise 2.1, the first step is to make a copy of Loan1 and use the editing commands of Turbo Pascal to make the necessary changes.

```
copy loan1.pas c2e2.pas
turbo c2e2.pas
```

In this exercise, you are asked to remove the line of the main program that calls `WriteTotals` (see line 187 in Fig. 2.2 of your text). There are several other lines in the program that contain the name `WriteTotals`. Be sure that you remove the one in the main program, as shown in Fig. 2.2 -- this location is three lines from the end of the program.

Begin by moving the cursor to the beginning of the line you want to delete. You can do this by using <PgDn> and the arrow keys, as you did in Exercise 2.1. If your computer has a mouse, you can also use the *scroll bar* at the right-hand side of the screen to scroll through the program. You can move the cursor to any location on the screen by simply clicking the mouse at that location, instead of using the arrow keys.

After you have moved to the line to be deleted, your cursor will be in this position:

```
  WriteTotals;
```

Now delete this line one character at a time by pressing the <Del> key. Eventually the entire line will disappear, and the following line will move up to take its place.

Next, you need to change the comment that appears on line 185 of Fig. 2.2 (this is two lines above the line you just deleted). In the original program, this comment reads

```
{ write totals and exit program }
```

You want to remove the "write totals" part of this comment, because your new program will no longer display the totals. Use the arrow keys to move the cursor to the beginning of the words you want to delete. Your cursor will be in this position:

```
{ write totals and exit program }
```

Now you can delete letters, one at a time, by pressing <Del>. After you have finished deleting "write totals and", your line will look like this:

```
{ exit program }
```

This completes the changes called for in Exercise 2.2. Check your work by comparing what you see on the screen with the lines shown in Fig. 2.5 of your text. If everything is correct, compile your new program. As before, you can do this by selecting Compile from the Compile menu. (From now on, we will sometimes write menu selection instructions like this in an abbreviated form as Compile | Compile.) Then select Run | Run to execute the program. Check the output produced by your program to be sure it is what you intended (see p. 24 of your text).

Remember to select File | Save to save your program before leaving Turbo Pascal. If you ever forget this step, Turbo Pascal will warn you that the program has been modified and ask whether you want to save it. If you get this message, type y to save the new version of the program (or n if you don't want to save the changes).

Exercise 2.3

This exercise asks you to create another new program named C2E3. Begin in the same way as you did before:

```
copy loan1.pas c2e3.pas
turbo c2e3.pas
```

The changes you will make in this exercise are very similar to the ones you did in Exercise 2.2. You want to delete the line that contains WriteHeadings (line 175 in Fig. 2.2 in your text), and change the related comment on line 172. You also want to delete the lines that contain begin, WriteBalance, and end (lines 180, 182, and 183), and change the related comment on line 177.

To accomplish this, you can proceed in the same way as you did in Exercise 2.2. First use <PgDn> and the arrow keys to move the cursor to the line in the main program that contains WriteHeadings. Then use <Del> to delete this line, one character at a time. Use the arrow keys to move the cursor to the line that contains the related comment, and then to the beginning of the words you want to delete. Use <Del> to delete the appropriate letters and words from the comment, so that it matches the comment shown in Fig. 2.6.

You could follow the same procedure to delete the other lines and change the associated comment. However, there is another method that you may find easier to use in some situations. Suppose that you want to delete the two lines that contain WriteBalance and end. First move the cursor to the beginning of the lines that you want to delete, as shown here:

```
for Month := 1 to 12 do
   begin
      ComputeNewBalance;
☐     WriteBalance
   end;
```

Hold down the <Shift> key and use the arrow keys to move the cursor past the lines to be deleted. Notice that the lines you pass over become highlighted, like this:

```
for Month := 1 to 12 do
   begin
      ComputeNewBalance;
      WriteBalance
   end;
☐
```

Now select Clear from the Edit menu, and the highlighted lines will disappear.

You can delete single lines, or even parts of lines, in this same way (instead of using the <Del> key). This method is especially easy to use if you have a mouse. In that case, you can highlight the characters or lines you want to delete by dragging the mouse across them, instead of using <Shift> and the arrow keys.

After you have made the other changes called for in the exercise, compare your new program with the lines shown in Fig. 2.6. If everything is correct, compile and run your new program, and check the results against those described in the text.

Exercise 2.4

This exercise asks you to make a more extensive change in the program Loan1, producing a new program named C2E4. The original version of the main program for Loan1 appears in Fig. 2.2 of your text. You want the main program for C2E4 to be as shown below; the annotations indicate which lines need to be changed or added to produce this version.

```
changed→    { initialize variables and write headings for months 1-6 }

            Initialize;
            WriteHeadings;

changed→    { compute and write balances for months 1-6 }

changed→    for Month := 1 to 6 do
               begin
                  ComputeNewBalance;
                  WriteBalance
               end;

added→      { write headings for months 7-12 }
added→
added→      WriteHeadings;
added→
added→      { compute and write balances for months 7-12 }
added→
added→      for Month := 7 to 12 do
added→         begin
added→            ComputeNewBalance;
added→            WriteBalance
added→         end;
added→

            { write totals and exit program }

            WriteTotals;
            CleanUp
```

Begin in the same way as in the previous exercises.

```
copy loan1.pas c2e4.pas
turbo c2e4.pas
```

Now move the cursor to the line in the existing program that contains the `for` statement.

     ☐ `for Month := 1 to 12 do`

Change the `12` in this line to `6`, just as you did in Exercise 2.1.
    Next move the cursor to this comment line

     `{ compute and write balances for each month of the loan }`

You can delete `"each month of the loan"` by pressing the <Del> key several times. Or, if you prefer, you can highlight these words (by using <Shift> and the arrow keys or by dragging the mouse) and then select Edit | Clear to delete them. Then type the text you want to insert (`"months 1-6"`). The result should look like this:

     `{ compute and write balances for months 1-6 }`

You can use almost exactly the same procedure to change the other comment line. This time, there is nothing that needs to be deleted. Move the cursor to the place where you want the insertion to go.

     `{ initialize variables and write headings }`

Then type `"for months 1-6 "`.
    Now you need to add several new lines to the program, as shown at the beginning of this discussion. Move the cursor to the place in the program where you want the new lines to go, as shown here:

```
for Month := 1 to 6 do
  begin
    ComputeNewBalance;
    WriteBalance
  end;

  { write totals and exit program }
```

Now begin typing the lines you want to insert. At the end of each line, you can press <Enter> and continue with the next line, just as though you were typing lines on a typewriter. Pressing <Enter> twice in a row gives you a blank line. Notice that Turbo Pascal automatically starts each line in the same column as the previous line. If necessary, you can use the space bar and the backspace key to make sure the statements line up properly.

It is easy to make mistakes when you are typing a long insertion. If you notice a mistake, you can backspace and correct it. Or you can move the cursor back and correct the error by using the same editing commands you have already learned.

If you discover that you are making an insertion in the wrong place, you may want to cancel it and start over. In that case, you can select Edit | Undo to "undo" the insertion. If you have inserted several lines, you will need to repeat the Edit | Undo for each inserted line you want to undo. You can also use this method to undo the effect of other editing operations, such as deletions and cursor movements. (If you are using an earlier version of Turbo Pascal, this feature may not be available.)

After you have finished making all of the changes to C2E4.PAS, compare your program with the lines shown in Fig. 2.7 of your text. Then compile and run your new program.

Cutting, Copying, and Pasting

In Exercise 2.3, you learned how to highlight parts of the program by using <Shift> and the arrow keys (or by dragging the mouse). You could then delete these parts of the program by selecting Edit | Clear. If you wanted to move the text you are deleting to another location in the program, you could use Edit | Cut instead of Edit | Clear. In that case, the text being deleted would be saved in a special place called the *clipboard*. You could then move the cursor to the new location and insert the lines from the clipboard by selecting Edit | Paste. Edit | Copy works just like Edit | Cut, except that the highlighted text is not deleted from its original location. However, it is placed on the clipboard so that it can be pasted into another location.

These techniques can save you a lot of retyping when you want to move large blocks of text from one place to another. They can also be useful if you are adding statements to a program that are similar to ones that already exist. For example, in Exercise 2.4 the for loop that you added was almost identical to the one that already existed. You might have chosen to copy the existing loop, paste it into the new location, and then make the necessary changes. This would have involved less typing (and less chance of error) than retyping the loop.

If you are interested, you may want to experiment with these commands now. Or you may prefer to simply remember that the commands are available, and look back at this section when you have a need to use them later.

Exercises 2.5 - 2.7

You can do these exercises by using the same techniques you have already learned. Begin by thinking about how you want to change the program -- for example, which lines you want to add, modify, or delete. Then look for similarities between these changes and the ones you performed in the preceding exercises. Be sure to compile and run your modified program, to make certain that it does what you intended. If you run into problems, come back to these exercises after you have read the discussion in your text about how to find errors in programs.

Exercise 2.8

In this exercise, you will begin learning how to find errors in programs. The exercise first asks you to change the `for` statement of the program C2E1 (the one you created while doing Exercise 2.1) from

```
for Month := 1 to 6 do
```

to

```
for Month := 1 to y do
```

This creates an error that you will find when you try to compile the program.

Suppose that we decide to call the program created in this exercise C2E8. Begin in the same way as in previous exercises:

```
copy c2e1.pas c2e8.pas
turbo c2e8.pas
```

Make the desired change in the `for` statement, and then use <PgUp> to move the cursor to another part of the program. (This is not really necessary, but it will help you to see how Turbo Pascal locates the error for you.) When you attempt to compile the program, you will see the error message

```
Error 3: Unknown identifier.
```

appear at the top of the screen. (The number 3 is a method that Turbo Pascal uses to identify its error messages -- it does not mean that there are three errors in the program.)

Notice that the cursor is positioned at the "unknown identifier" `y`. This shows you where the error is located, and also makes it easy to correct the problem. Do this now, by deleting the `y` and replacing it by `6`. Then recompile the program to be sure that everything is correct.

Exercise 2.9

In this exercise, you will create another common kind of compilation error -- a missing semicolon. Enter the commands

```
copy c2e1.pas c2e9.pas
turbo c2e9.pas
```

and delete the semicolon following `ComputeNewBalance`. As before, use <PgUp> to move to another part of the program before you try to compile it. This time, you will get the error message

```
Error 85: ";" expected.
```

The compiler has done a good job of finding the problem. Notice, however, that the cursor is positioned at the beginning of the next line of the program, not at the end of the line where you removed the semicolon.

Correct the error by inserting the missing semicolon and recompile the program. Notice that the error message disappears as soon as you press any key to begin the correction. If you want to see the error message again, you can select "Show last compiler error" from the Search menu.

Exercise 2.10

This exercise asks you to delete the line of C2E1 that contains `end`. Be sure that you delete the `"end;"` following the line that contains `WriteBalance` (see Fig. 2.4), *not* the `"end."` that appears as the last line of the file. When you try to compile the program, you will get the error message

```
Error 85: ";" expected.
```

and the cursor will be left in this position:

```
for Month := 1 to 6 do
   begin
      ComputeNewBalance;
      WriteBalance

{ write totals and exit program }

WriteTotals;
CleanUp
```

This time, the compiler did not do as good a job of diagnosing the problem. The missing `end` should be between the lines that contain `WriteBalance` and `WriteTotals`. However, the compiler had no way of knowing that there was supposed to be an `end` there. It did detect that there was no semicolon between `WriteBalance` and `WriteTotals`, which caused the error message.

When you are correcting compilation errors, it is important to think about what you intended the statements to do, instead of just automatically making corrections as indicated by the compiler. In this situation, if you simply inserted a semicolon after `WriteBalance` and tried to recompile the program, you would get another compilation error. Even if the program did compile correctly (after fixing a series of errors), it would do something very different from what you intended.

Printing a Program Listing

Sometimes you may want to print out a listing of your program so you can look at it away from the computer (or hand it in as part of a homework assignment). You can print such a listing by selecting File | Print. Your instructor will show you where to pick up the printed output that is created.

Exercises 2.11 - 2.13

These exercises ask you to find and correct compilation errors in programs. You can do this using the same methods we discussed for Exercises 2.8 through 2.10. First compile the program to see what error messages you get. After correcting the compilation errors, recompile the program and run it to be sure that it works correctly. For example, C2E11 is a program that might have been produced while attempting Exercise 2.1. After correcting the compilation errors, run C2E11 and compare the results with those described for Exercise 2.1.

Exercise 2.14

This exercise asks you to find a logic error in the program C2E14.PAS, which is already stored on your disk. Follow the same procedure that is described in your text in the discussions of Figs. 2.8 and 2.9. First compile and run the program, and compare the output it produces with what the program is supposed to do. The exercise says that C2E14 is a program that might have been produced while attempting Exercise 2.1. Therefore, you should compare the output from C2E14 with the correct output for Exercise 2.1 (shown in Fig. 2.3 in your text).

The next step is to examine the main program of C2E14 to determine why it produced this incorrect output. As usual, you can press <Enter> at the end of the program to return to the Turbo Pascal screen that shows the program itself. Use <PgDn> to move to the main program, as you did in the previous exercises. You may find it useful to go through the statements in the main program, one at a time, as described in the text. (This is called *tracing* the execution of the program.)

If you want to go back and look at the output from the program again, it is not necessary to rerun the program. You can switch back to the screen that displays the output by selecting "User screen" from the Debug menu. (If you are using an earlier version of Turbo Pascal, you may find the "User screen" choice under the Window menu instead.) After looking at the output, you can return to the Turbo Pascal screen by pressing any key.

After you figure out what is wrong with the main program, correct the errors. Then recompile the program and run it again, to be sure that it works correctly.

Exercises 2.15 - 2.17

These exercises ask you to find and correct logic errors in other programs. Follow the same procedure as for Exercise 2.14. First compile and run the program, and compare the output with what the program is supposed to do. (Notice that the intended output is different from one exercise to another.) Then examine the main program carefully to find the logic errors it contains. As in Exercise 2.14, you may want to trace the execution of the main program, one statement at a time.

Remember to recompile the program and run it again after making corrections, to be sure that you have found all of the errors.

Removing Unneeded Files

As you did the exercises for this chapter, you created many new Pascal programs (.PAS files). As you made changes in programs, you also created many backup versions (.BAK files). All these files take up space on your disk -- eventually, the disk will fill up and you will have to change to a new one. You can help delay this problem by removing files that you no longer need.

You will probably want to keep the final version of each program for future reference. However, once you have completed work on a program, you probably do not need the backup version. You can remove these unneeded files by using the DOS erase command. For example, you can enter

```
erase c2e1.bak
```

to remove the backup version of program C2E1.

You could remove the backup versions of programs C2E2 through C2E17 by entering similar commands, one at a time. However, there is an easier way to accomplish this. Enter the command

```
erase *.bak
```

The * is a *wildcard* that matches any string of characters. Thus *.bak matches all file names that end in .BAK. This erase command removes all such files from the directory you are currently working in. Do this now, in order to be sure that you have enough disk space for the exercises in the next chapter.

Warning

Be very careful when using wildcards to remove files. If you should accidentally type *.pas instead of *.bak, you would erase all of your Pascal programs. If you accidentally typed *.*, you might erase all of the files on your disk!

CHAPTER

3

As you do the exercises in this chapter, you will use many of the same DOS commands and Turbo Pascal menus that you learned about in Chapters 1 and 2. You may find it useful to glance back over these previous exercises, looking for similarities to the exercise you are currently doing. Our discussions of the exercises in this chapter will focus on some new techniques that can make editing programs easier.

For convenience, the Turbo Pascal menus and the most commonly used DOS commands are summarized in "quick reference" sections at the end of this lab manual.

Changing Directories

Begin by following the same "getting started" procedure as in previous chapters. Boot the system, if necessary, and insert your program disk into drive A. (You will have to perform these steps each time you use the computer. From now on, we will not repeat the instructions at the start of each chapter.) Before beginning the exercises in Chapter 3, remember to change to the directory CHAP3 by entering the command

        cd chap3

If you have already been working in the directory CHAP2 (for example, if you have just been doing exercises from Chapter 2), you will need to change back to the main directory on your disk by entering

        cd \

before entering the cd chap3. (See the discussion of directories at the beginning of Chapter 2 of this lab manual.)

Now use the command dir to list the contents of the directory CHAP3. You should see a listing like

        Directory of A:\CHAP3

        C3E3   PAS   7033   3-09-94   11:50a
        LOAN1   PAS   7300   3-09-94   11:50a

Exercise 3.1

This exercise asks you to make a change in the procedure named `WriteTotals`. You could find this procedure by using <PgDn> repeatedly, as you did in Chapter 2. You would examine each page, looking for the procedure header for `WriteTotals`. However, there is a faster way to accomplish this.

After you have started Turbo Pascal, select Find from the Search menu. A *dialog box* that looks like this will appear on your screen.

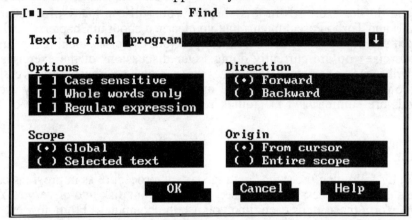

As you can see, there are a lot of choices that you can make in this box. You may want to read about some of these options in the Turbo Pascal manual later on. For now, however, all you need to do is type the text you want to find. The cursor should be at the beginning of the section marked "Text to find". (If it is not, press <Tab> several times until the cursor reaches this section.) Now type `WriteTotals` in the box and press <Enter>. (It is not necessary to erase the text that is initially in the box -- that is just Turbo Pascal's guess about what you want.)

After you type the text to find and press <Enter>, the box will disappear. Your cursor will automatically move to the first line in the file that contains the text you specified. In this case, that line is the header for the procedure `WriteTotals`. (You will notice that the `WriteTotals` in this line is now highlighted. However, this is of no concern -- the highlighting will disappear as soon as you press another key.)

Now that you have found the procedure `WriteTotals`, you are ready to make the desired changes. In this exercise, for example, you will probably want to delete the `writeln` statement that writes the totals and replace it with several `writeln` statements of your own. As always, remember to test the modified version of the program to be sure that it does what you intended.

Leaving Turbo Pascal without Changing the Program

When you are editing a program, you may occasionally decide that you are making the wrong changes. In that case, you might want to exit from Turbo Pascal and leave the program as it originally was. You can do this by selecting File | Exit without saving the program. Turbo Pascal will warn you that the program has been modified, and ask whether you want to save it. Type n and the program file will be left unchanged.

If you have already saved changes to a program, remember that the most recent previous version is still available in a .BAK file. For example, suppose that you have made some changes to C3E1 and then decide that those changes were a mistake. You can restore the previous version by entering the command

```
copy c3e1.bak c3e1.pas
```

Exercise 3.2

This exercise asks you to make a change in the following lines of the program:

```
writeln('TOTAL INTEREST PAID   = ', TotalInterestPaid:8:2);
writeln('TOTAL INTEREST EARNED = ', TotalInterestEarned:8:2);
```

You can find these lines by using the same operation that you learned in Exercise 3.1. Select Find from the Search menu and type the text

```
TOTAL INTEREST PAID
```

in the dialog box; remember to press <Enter> after typing this text. The cursor will move to a line that looks like this:

```
TotalInterestPaid : real;      { total interest paid }
```

This is the first line in the program that contains the text you typed (notice that uppercase and lowercase letters are considered the same). However, this line is not the one you want. To look for the next matching line, select "Search again" from the Search menu. This time, the cursor will move to the first of the two lines you need to change for this exercise.

Exercise 3.3

Notice that this exercise involves making changes to a file C3E3.PAS that already exists in the directory CHAP3. It is *not* necessary to copy LOAN1.PAS in order to create this file.

Exercise 3.3 requires making changes in two different areas of the program. You need to add a declaration of a new variable CashNeeded to the declaration section of the program. You also need to remove the procedure WriteTotals and replace it with a new procedure WriteCashNeeded that you have written.

You can find the parts of the program to be changed by using Search | Find as before. The declaration section of the program begins with var (see Fig. 3.4 in your text). You can move to this line by typing var in the dialog box for the Find operation. After you add the new variable declaration, you can find the procedure `WriteTotals` in the same way you did in Exercise 3.1.

Next you need to delete the procedure `WriteTotals`, so that you can replace it with your new procedure `WriteCashNeeded`. The easiest way to do this is to use the Edit | Clear operation that you learned about in Exercise 2.3. First move the cursor to the beginning of the first line you want to delete. Highlight all of the lines of the procedure `WriteTotals` by holding down the <Shift> key and using the arrow keys to move the cursor. (Remember that you can also do this by dragging the mouse, if your computer has one.) Then select Edit | Clear to delete these lines.

Finally, insert your new procedure `WriteCashNeeded`, and compile and test the program.

Exercise 3.4

In this exercise, you need to make related changes to two different procedures -- `WriteBalance` and `WriteHeadings`. Suppose that you decide to change `WriteBalance` first. As before, you can use Search | Find (typing `WriteBalance` in the dialog box) to locate this procedure.

After making the necessary change, you are ready to move to the procedure `WriteHeadings`. Use Search | Find again (searching for `WriteHeadings`). You will find the cursor at the line

```
WriteHeadings;
```

which is the line in the main program that calls the procedure `WriteHeadings`. This is not the part of the program that you want to change. As before, you can repeat the search (looking for another line that contains `WriteHeadings`) by selecting "Search again" from the Search menu. This time, you will see a box with the message "Search string not found".

You are sure that this program contains a procedure named `WriteHeadings` -- what has gone wrong? Press <Enter> to make the error message disappear. Now select Search | Find again and look at the dialog box.

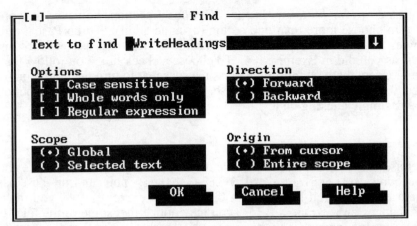

Notice that the box is divided into several sections marked "Text to find", "Options", "Direction", and so on. The cursor is positioned in the section marked "Text to find". Press <Tab> once and the cursor will move to the next section ("Options"). (On some keyboards, the <Tab> key may be marked →⊣ .) Continue to press <Tab> until the cursor reaches the "Origin" section.

This section contains two choices -- "From cursor" and "Entire scope". Notice that "From cursor" has a dot by it, indicating that this choice is selected. This means that the search for the text you type begins where the cursor is currently positioned. Because the "Forward" choice is selected in the "Direction" section, the search continues forward until the end of the program is reached. In the search you just performed, the cursor was positioned in the procedure WriteBalance. However, the procedure WriteHeadings occurs in the program *before* WriteBalance. This explains why your search was not successful.

Now press the ↓ key once. Notice that the dialog box changes so that "Entire scope" is selected. This means that the search will begin at the start of the program. Now press <Enter> to begin the search, and you will find the procedure WriteHeadings that you were looking for. Make the needed changes in this procedure, and then compile and test your program.

More about Dialog Boxes

You can make other choices in a dialog box using methods like those you learned in Exercise 3.4. For example, you might choose "Backward" in the "Direction" section to search backwards from the current cursor position. You might choose "Case sensitive" in the "Options" section to specify that uppercase and lowercase letters should be considered different during the search.

The "Options" section is different from the other sections in this dialog box. In the other sections, only one choice at a time can be selected -- for example, it would make no sense to choose both "Forward" and "Backward". Turbo Pascal refers to these choices as *radio buttons*. In the "Options" section, however, it would be meaningful to choose more than one option (or none at all). Turbo Pascal refers to these choices as *check boxes*. To choose a radio button, you use <Tab> and the arrow keys, as you did in Exercise 3.4. To choose a check box, you follow the same procedure -- except that you must then press the spacebar to turn the option on (or off, if it is already on). If you are using a mouse, you can choose either a radio button or a check box by simply clicking on it.

Exercise 3.5

In this exercise you will need to add a declaration of a new variable, and make changes in the procedures `WriteBalance` and `WriteHeadings`. You can find these parts of the program using Search | Find, as in the previous exercises. As you make the necessary changes in `WriteHeadings`, you may notice that some of the lines of the program become too long to fit on the screen. Notice that Turbo Pascal automatically takes care of this for you, by "scrolling" the screen from left to right as you type text or move the cursor.

When you are working with long lines, it may be inconvenient to move around by using the arrow keys alone. You can move quickly to the beginning of a line by pressing the key marked <Home>. Similarly, the <End> key will take you directly to the end of a line.

Exercise 3.6

In this exercise, you make changes to some of the constant definitions in the program. There are several different ways that you might go about doing this. You could use <PgDn> to look through the program until you find the constant definitions. You could find the constant definitions by using Search | Find and entering the text `const` in the dialog box (notice that you will need to repeat the search to get to the right place). In either of these cases, you would then use <Del> to remove the old constant values and then type in the new values.

A different approach would allow you to combine the searching and replacing of values into a single operation. For example, suppose that you want to change the line

```
PaymentAmount = 263.05;        { amount of monthly payment }
```

so that it reads

```
PaymentAmount = 250.00;        { amount of monthly payment }
```

If you select Replace from the Search menu, you will see a dialog box similar to the one you used with Find. Type `263.05` in the "Text to find" section; then press <Tab> to move to the "New text" section and type `250.00`. When you press <Enter>, Turbo Pascal will find the line with `263.05` and ask you to confirm that this is the occurrence that you want to replace. You can follow a similar procedure with the other values you want to change. (You will probably want to choose the "Entire scope" radio button, as you did in Exercise 3.4.)

As you continue to use Turbo Pascal, you will often find that there are several different ways to accomplish the same thing. You may want to try out different commands to become familiar with what they do, and then use whatever method seems easiest to you. If you need more details or explanation about a command or dialog box, you can look in the Turbo Pascal manual or use the online Help function. (You can ask for help at any time while using Turbo Pascal by pressing <F1>.)

Exercise 3.7

In this exercise, you change Loan1 so that the variable `SavingsBalance` is not initialized properly. Notice that the program compiles without any errors, and appears to run normally. However, the results are incorrect.

It is easy for even experienced programmers to forget to initialize variables. Be sure to check for this in the programs you write.

Exercise 3.9

In this exercise, you create your first complete new program. As the text describes, you will need to write procedures, variable declarations, and constant definitions to go with the main program shown in Fig. 3.12(b). Then you will combine these parts (in the correct order) to form your complete program.

You will probably find it easiest to write the program out on paper first, instead of trying to compose it at the computer. When you are ready to type the program in, enter the command

```
turbo savings.pas
```

Because there is no file named SAVINGS.PAS in your directory, this command creates a new (empty) file to receive your program. (If you leave out the extension .pas, Turbo Pascal will automatically supply it for you. However, it is a good habit always to use full file names, including the extension.) The cursor is positioned at the beginning of the first (empty) line on your screen. Now begin typing your program. As before, you can correct typing errors by backspacing; or you can go back later and use editing commands to correct them.

You will almost certainly get errors when you try to compile and run your new program. (It is rare for even highly experienced programmers to write a program that runs perfectly the first time.) Find and correct the compilation errors, using the same methods you learned in Chapter 2. Then carefully compare the output your program produces with the desired output shown in Fig. 3.11 of your text. Fix any logic errors that you find in the program.

Then congratulate yourself on finishing your first new program!

CHAPTER

4

In previous chapters, we have commented on every exercise that involved using the computer. As you did those exercises, you were learning many different things about how to edit and run programs. Now you have learned most of the commands and other mechanical details that you will need in this course. From now on, we will comment only on those exercises and other parts of the text that involve new techniques. If you have trouble seeing how to do one of the other exercises, try glancing back over the preceding chapters. If you can find an earlier exercise that does something similar, you can probably apply the same techniques to your current task.

Getting the Directory for Chapter 4

All of the files you have worked with so far have been on your program disk, which you inserted in drive A each time you used the computer. This disk contained separate directories for Chapter 2 and Chapter 3. The directories for Chapter 4 and the later chapters were left out to simplify things for you in Chapters 1-3. Now it is time to get the directory you will need for the exercises in Chapter 4. You will be getting the files for Chapter 4 from a program directory that was set up for your class to use. The contents of this directory look like

```
CHAP1      <DIR>      3-09-94    1:02p
CHAP2      <DIR>      3-09-94    1:02p
CHAP3      <DIR>      3-09-94    1:02p
CHAP4      <DIR>      3-09-94    1:02p
CHAP5      <DIR>      3-09-94    1:03p
CHAP6      <DIR>      3-09-94    1:03p
CHAP7      <DIR>      3-09-94    1:03p
CHAP8      <DIR>      3-09-94    1:03p
CHAP9      <DIR>      3-09-94    1:04p
CHAP10     <DIR>      3-09-94    1:04p
CHAP11     <DIR>      3-09-94    1:04p
CHAP12     <DIR>      3-09-94    1:06p
CHAP13     <DIR>      3-09-94    1:06p
CHAP14     <DIR>      3-09-94    1:06p
DICTION    <DIR>      3-09-94    1:06p
```

Directories provide a useful way of organizing files. In the first three chapters of this text you have already worked with more than 30 different files, and there are many others in the later chapters. It would be very hard to keep track of these files if they were all stored in the same directory. To simplify things, we have stored files in different directories, one for each chapter of the text. There is also a directory named DICTION that contains dictionaries used by the anagram-finding programs.

You want to copy the directory CHAP4 (and all of the files it contains) to your program disk so that you can work with it. The exact method for doing this depends on how your laboratory is set up -- your instructor will tell you how to proceed. After you have copied the directory CHAP4, use the command cd to change to this directory and dir to list its contents. You should see a listing like

```
Directory of A:\CHAP4

C4E10     PAS     13725     3-09-94    11:50a
C4E11     PAS     13718     3-09-94    11:50a
C4E8      PAS     13329     3-09-94    11:50a
LOAN2     PAS     11916     3-09-94    11:50a
LOAN3     PAS     13722     3-09-94    11:50a
LOANDEBG  PAS     13717     3-09-94    11:50a
```

Exercise 4.6

In this exercise, you intentionally enter an invalid numeric value by typing T999 for the amount financed. When you do this, your program terminates with a run-time error. Turbo Pascal displays an error message ("Invalid numeric format") to tell you what happened. It also moves the cursor to the line in the program that was being executed when the error occurred. (In this case, that line is the readln statement that reads a value for Loan.AmountFinanced.)

Exercise 4.8

In this exercise, you intentionally run a program with an infinite (or unending) loop. Each time through the loop, the program displays savings and loan balances for one month. When you run this program, you will be asked for starting balances, interest rates, and payment amount. Enter the same values that you used when you did Exercise 4.3. As soon as you enter the payment amount, you will see a steady stream of lines displayed on your screen. The listing will not pause every 12 months, as it did when you ran Loan3. The program will keep running and displaying lines until you do something to stop it.

You can stop a program that is in an infinite loop by typing <Ctrl+Break>. (This means that you hold down the <Ctrl> key and press the <Break> key at the same time.) The program should stop running and you should see the Turbo Pascal screen reappear. If the program continues to run, try <Ctrl+Break> again.

This is an important technique to remember. As you write more complicated programs, you will sooner or later produce one with an error that leads to an infinite loop. Sometimes you will see a program that begins to run and then appears to stop suddenly, without returning you to the Turbo Pascal screen. Such a program is probably in an infinite loop; it appears to be doing nothing because it is not producing any output during the loop. You should be able to stop the program by typing <Ctrl+Break>. (If the program is waiting for you to enter input at the keyboard, you may need to enter the requested input before the <Ctrl+Break> takes effect.)

Debugging in Turbo Pascal

Turbo Pascal provides many features that can help you find errors in programs. When you typed <Ctrl+Break> to stop the program in Exercise 4.8, you saw a message that read "User break in C4E8.PAS ...". This means that the program was stopped at your request. The line number tells you which instruction in the program was being executed when you stopped it. If you have already exited from Turbo Pascal, run the program C4E8 again and stop it with <Ctrl+Break> so that you get this message. Now press <Enter>. The message will disappear and you will see the line of the program where execution was stopped, as shown here:

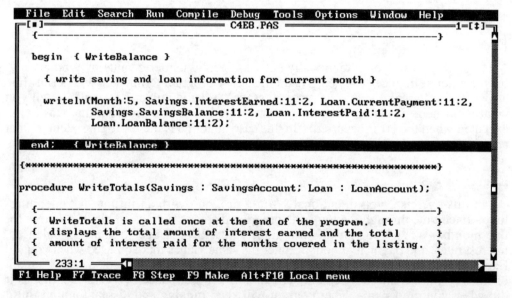

When Turbo Pascal interrupts execution of a program, it highlights the *next* line that would have been executed. In this example, the `end` statement of the procedure `WriteBalance` is highlighted. This means that the program was executing the last statement in that procedure (the `writeln`) when you typed <Ctrl+Break>. (It is possible that you may see a different line highlighted, if you happened to catch the program in a different place.)

Now let's see how we could use the debugger to find out more about this infinite loop. We are going to run the program in "slow motion", while watching the output that is being generated. Begin by selecting Output from the Debug menu. (If you are using an earlier version of Turbo Pascal, you may find Output under the Window menu instead.) Your screen will change to look something like this:

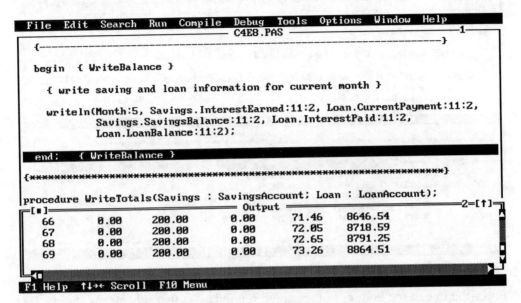

```
  File  Edit  Search  Run  Compile  Debug  Tools  Options  Window  Help
─────────────────────────────── C4E8.PAS ───────────────────────────1──
┌──────────────────────────────────────────────────────────────────┐
│ {─────────────────────────────────────────────────────────────────} │
│                                                                      │
│ begin  { WriteBalance }                                              │
│                                                                      │
│   { write saving and loan information for current month }            │
│                                                                      │
│   writeln(Month:5, Savings.InterestEarned:11:2, Loan.CurrentPayment:11:2,│
│           Savings.SavingsBalance:11:2, Loan.InterestPaid:11:2,       │
│           Loan.LoanBalance:11:2);                                    │
│                                                                      │
│ █end;   { WriteBalance }█████████████████████████████████████████    │
│                                                                      │
│{******************************************************************}  │
│                                                                      │
│ procedure WriteTotals(Savings : SavingsAccount; Loan : LoanAccount); │
│ ┌─[■]──────────────────────── Output ────────────────────────2=[↑]─┐ │
│ │   66      0.00    200.00      0.00     71.46    8646.54         │ │
│ │   67      0.00    200.00      0.00     72.05    8718.59         │ │
│ │   68      0.00    200.00      0.00     72.65    8791.25         │ │
│ │   69      0.00    200.00      0.00     73.26    8864.51         │ │
│ │◄                                                             ►│ │
│ └──────────────────────────────────────────────────────────────┘ │
└──────────────────────────────────────────────────────────────────┘
 F1 Help  ↑↓→← Scroll  F10 Menu
```

There is a new *window* titled "Output" at the bottom of the screen that shows the output generated so far. (The actual contents of your output window will be different, depending on exactly when you stopped the program.)

Turbo Pascal allows you to have many different windows open at the same time. However, only one window at a time can be *active*. Notice that the border and title of the output window are highlighted. This shows you that the output window is now the active window.

Any text that you type or editing commands that you select apply only to the active window. Suppose, for example, that you want to use the arrow keys to look at a different part of the program. In order to do this, you need to *activate* the window that contains the program. You can do this by selecting Window | Next, or by using the hot key <F6>. After you do this, your screen will look the same as it did after you stopped the program.

When you activated the program window, the output window disappeared. This window still exists. Unfortunately, it is now "underneath" the program window, so we can't see it. You can take care of this by selecting Window | Tile. This rearranges the windows so they will fit on the screen without overlapping. If you do this now, your screen will look like

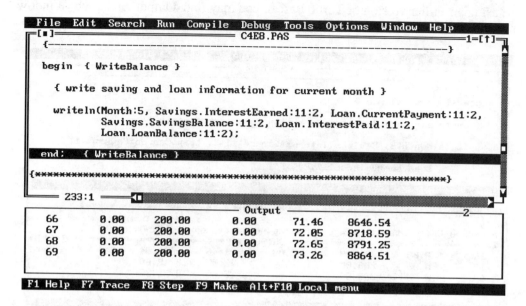

Now we are ready to resume running the program, one statement at a time. Press <F8> (the line at the bottom of the screen reminds you that this means Step). The program will execute one statement and stop again. As before, the highlighted line indicates the next statement to be executed. Press <F8> several more times, and you will be able to watch the execution of the while loop in the main program. Notice that a new line of output appears each time the procedure WriteBalance is called.

It seems that our program is stuck in this while loop. This would happen if the condition in the loop (Loan.LoanBalance > 0) always remains true. (A look at the loan balances being displayed in the output window confirms this -- the balances are increasing, instead of decreasing.) This gives us a clue about the possible cause of the problem. See the description of Exercise 4.8 in your text for more information about what is actually wrong with the program.

More Debugging Features

In this section, you will learn how to use the Turbo Pascal debugger to perform the same debugging operations that are illustrated in Fig. 4.14 of your text. As the text discusses, we want to look at the value of Savings.TotalInterestEarned after each call to the procedures Initialize and ComputeNewBalance.

The incorrect program that contains the error is stored in the file LOANDEBG.PAS. Start Turbo Pascal and compile this program. Then press <F8> to begin executing the program one statement at a time. (If you forget this hot key, you can accomplish the same thing by selecting Run | Step.) The execution point (indicated by a highlighted line) will move to the beginning of the main program. Press <F8> again, and the call to `Initialize` will be highlighted. (Remember that execution stops before this highlighted line is executed.) Press <F8> again; the procedure `Initialize` will be called, and will ask you to enter initial values for saving and loan balances, interest rates, and payment amount. Enter the following values, as shown in Fig. 4.13(a):

```
Starting savings balance        : 3000
Interest rate on savings (%)    : 6.5
Amount financed on loan         : 800
Interest rate on loan (%)       : 10
Monthly payment on loan         : 200
```

Now we are ready to look at the value of `Savings.TotalInterestEarned`. Turbo Pascal has a feature that allows us to "watch" the values of any variables or expressions we are interested in. Select "Add watch" from the Debug menu. (If you are using an earlier version of Turbo Pascal, you may need to select Debug | Watches | Add watch.) Type `Savings.TotalInterestEarned` in the dialog box that is presented, and then press <Enter>. You will see a Watch window appear at the bottom of the screen. This window shows that the current value of `Savings.TotalInterestEarned` is `0.0`. This corresponds to the first line of debugging output shown in Fig. 4.14(b).

Now we are going to continue to execute the program one step at a time. Select Window | Next to activate the program window; notice that this causes the watch window to disappear from view. As before, select Window | Tile to divide the screen between the program and watch windows. The result should look like this:

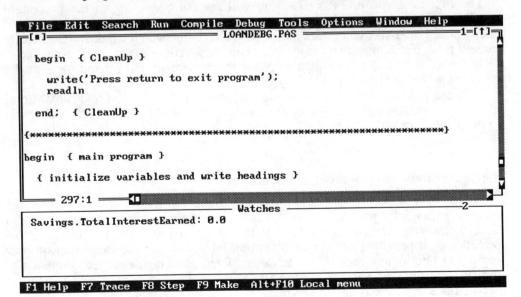

Now continue to step through the program by pressing <F8> to execute each statement. After the call to ComputeNewBalance is executed, you will see the value in the watch window change to 16.25. This value corresponds to the second line of debugging output in Fig. 4.14(b). Continue stepping through the program. After the next call to ComputeNewBalance, the value in the watch window will change to 21.921354167. This corresponds to the third line of debugging output in Fig. 4.14(b). Because Turbo Pascal had no way of knowing how you wanted the value formatted, it is displayed as 21.921354167 instead of being rounded to 21.92.

As the text describes, this value is in error -- it should be 31.50 (to two decimal places). Thus we know that the error must occur during the second call to ComputeNewBalance. In this case, the procedure ComputeNewBalance is simple enough that we can find the error by looking at the statements it contains. With more complicated procedures, however, this might be difficult to do. Let's see how we could use the debugger to find out more about what went wrong.

Restart the program at the beginning by selecting "Program reset" from the Run menu. Begin executing the program again, one statement at a time, by using <F8> as before. Enter the same initial data values when they are requested by the program. This time, however, stop just before the second call to ComputeNewBalance. At this time, the line that contains ComputeNewBalance will be highlighted, and the value in the watch window will be 16.25, as before. You know that the next procedure call will produce an incorrect value. To see what happens inside this procedure, press <F7> (Trace) instead of <F8> (Step). Tracing is similar to stepping, except that it traces execution into procedures instead of treating a procedure call as a single statement.

The first time you press <F7>, you will see the beginning of the procedure ComputeNewBalance. Continue to press <F7> to trace through this procedure, one statement at a time. As you do so, notice the value in the watch window. Eventually you will reach a statement that causes Savings.TotalInterestEarned to change to the incorrect value. You can then examine this statement and related parts of the procedure to find the problem.

This example has shown you how to use some of the simplest and most useful debugging commands. For a description of more advanced features of the debugger, see the Turbo Pascal manuals.

The Integrated Development Environment

As you have seen, Turbo Pascal provides support for many different parts of the program development process. If you get compilation errors or run-time errors, Turbo Pascal takes you directly to the part of the program involved so you can make corrections. It provides debugging tools that let you watch the execution of your program to find logic errors. More advanced features of the debugger allow you to modify the values of variables during execution of the program, and to stop at specified places in the program. When you have detected an error, you can make corrections and try the program again. You can perform all of these operations without ever leaving Turbo Pascal.

This Integrated Development Environment, or IDE, is one of the main advantages of using Turbo Pascal. If you were programming on a different system, you would probably have to use a separate text editor, compiler, and debugger. If you got a compilation error, you would have to leave the compiler and start the text editor in order to make corrections. If you found an error during debugging, you would have to make corrections with the editor, then use the compiler, and then try the debugger again. These separate pieces of software would probably not work together as well as the features of the IDE. The whole process might be much more difficult and time-consuming.

Some of the features of the Turbo Pascal IDE are summarized in a "quick reference" section at the end of this manual. If you want to learn more, the Turbo Pascal manuals are an excellent source of information.

CHAPTER

5

Before you begin the exercises in this chapter, you must get the directory that contains the files you need. You can do this by following the same procedure you learned at the beginning of Chapter 4. You will need to perform a similar operation at the beginning of each of the following chapters. From now on, we will not repeat this reminder each time.

Exercise 5.4

In this exercise, you write a program that calls the procedures `ReadMessage` and `WriteMessage`. These procedures are stored in files named `READMSG.PAS` and `WRITEMSG.PAS` in the directory `CHAP5`.

In Chapter 2, we discussed how to copy a block of text and paste it into another part of the program. You can also copy and paste blocks between different programs. Start Turbo Pascal and type your new program, as you have done before. However, do not include the definitions of the procedures `ReadMessage` and `WriteMessage`. Now select File | Open. Type the name `readmsg.pas` in the dialog box that appears, and press <Enter>.

When you do this, a new window will open on your screen; this window contains the procedure from `READMSG.PAS`. When the window opens, the cursor is at the beginning of the first line. Hold down the <Shift> key and use ↓ to move to the last line of the procedure. (Notice that this highlights a block of text that contains the procedure definition. You can also accomplish this highlighting by dragging the mouse, if your computer has one.) Select Edit | Copy to copy this block and save it on the clipboard. Now you are finished with the file `READMSG.PAS` -- close this window by selecting Window | Close. (When you select from the Window menu, be careful to choose "Close", not "Close all".)

Closing the `READMSG.PAS` window takes you back to the window that contains your program. Move the cursor to the place where you want the definition of the procedure `ReadMessage` to appear. Then select Edit | Paste to paste the block of text from the clipboard at this location. The block will remain highlighted after you paste it. This should cause no problem. However, if you prefer you can remove the highlighting. To do this, first move the cursor out of the highlighted block; then hold down <Shift> and press ↓ followed by ↑. (If you have a mouse, you can also do this by clicking anywhere in the program window.)

Now use the same method to copy the procedure from WRITEMSG.PAS and paste it into your program. You can always use this technique to move procedures (or other Pascal code) from one program to another. In a later chapter, you will also learn how to have the compiler include procedures like this directly, without copying and pasting.

Exercise 5.6

As part of this exercise, you need to create new files named EKEY and DKEY that contain enciphering and deciphering keys. You can create these files with Turbo Pascal, in the same way that you have created program files. For example, you can start Turbo Pascal and create a new file named EKEY with the command

```
turbo ekey.
```

The period (.) at the end of the file name is part of the command. Remember that Pascal assumes file names end with the extension .PAS. If you simply typed the command "turbo ekey" (without the period), Turbo Pascal would create a file named EKEY.PAS.

After starting Turbo Pascal, you can type the contents of the file you are creating and save it, just as you have done with programs. Similarly, you can create the file DKEY by using the command

```
turbo dkey.
```

Exercise 5.7

As the text describes, Turbo Pascal uses the assign statement to associate a file variable with the name of a disk file. You can change the program so that it reads the enciphering key from the file ENCODE by simply changing the assign statement to look like

```
assign(EKEY,'ENCODE');
```

A similar change will allow the program to read the deciphering key from the file DECODE.

CHAPTER

6

Exercise 6.5

In this exercise, you write a program that creates a file named MSGOUT. After running the program, you need to examine the contents of MSGOUT to be sure that the program worked properly. You can look at the contents of this file using Turbo Pascal by entering the command

```
turbo msgout.
```

Be sure to include the period at the end of the file name, so Turbo Pascal knows you mean the file MSGOUT, not MSGOUT.PAS. (See the discussion of Exercise 5.6.) If you want to print the file so that you can look at it away from the computer (or hand it in), you can select File | Print just as you did to print listings of programs.

Placement of Variable Declarations

As the text mentions (p. 134), some compilers allow variable declarations to be placed after the declarations of procedures and functions. This can help avoid accidental references to global variables. Turbo Pascal does allow this. In fact, it allows the declarations of constants, types, variables, procedures, and functions to appear in any order. These parts of the program can also be repeated as many times as desired. For example, it is possible to define some constants, types, and variables; then declare procedures and functions; and then define more constants, types, and variables.

Value of maxint

The value of maxint in Turbo Pascal is 32,767. The smallest negative integer is -32,768. Unfortunately, these limits are too small for some applications. It is not unusual to write a program that needs to deal with integers larger than 32,767. To allow for this, Turbo Pascal supports another integer data type named longint. Variables of type longint can be used in the same way as variables of type integer. However, longint variables can take on values from -2,147,483,648 to 2,147,483,647. There are also other integer types in Turbo Pascal: shortint (range of values from -128 to 127), byte (from 0 to 255), and word (from 0 to 65,535).

When the value of a variable goes outside its allowable range, we say that *overflow* has occurred. Normally, you will not get an error message in this situation. However, the value stored in the variable will be incorrect. For example, an `integer` variable that exceeds the value of `maxint` (32,767) will probably be transformed into a large negative value. If you suspect such a problem, you can request that Turbo Pascal check for overflow. To do this, select Options | Compiler and choose "Overflow checking" in the dialog box that appears.

CHAPTER

7

Exercise 7.2

In this exercise, you intentionally create a program that has a subscript out of range when it runs. As the text mentions, this kind of error can cause almost any kind of program behavior. You may see strange characters or colors appearing on your screen, the program may go into an infinite loop or appear to stop running, or you may get an error message that seems to have nothing to do with the actual error. It may be necessary to use <Ctrl+Break> to stop the program. Whenever you see behavior like this in a program you are debugging, you should suspect a subscript out of range.

If you request it, Turbo Pascal will check for subscripts out of range and give more helpful error messages. To specify this, select Options | Compiler and choose "Range checking" in the dialog box that appears. Then compile and run the program again, to see what happens.

CHAPTER
8

Exercise 8.1

Each time you run the program Solve, it displays a different cryptogram. As the text discusses, these cryptograms are read from a file named CRYPTO. Another file named CCOUNT is used to keep track of which cryptograms have already been displayed. There is also a file named CCOUNTI that can be used to initialize CCOUNT so that Solve will start over with the first cryptogram in CRYPTO. If you want to go back to the first cryptogram (for example, if you want to repeat Exercise 1.5 from Chapter 1), you can do this by entering the command

```
copy ccounti ccount
```

before you run Solve.

Nonstandard Constant Definitions

As the text discusses (p. 189), a constant definition of the form

```
Bell = chr(7);
```

is not allowed in standard Pascal. However, Turbo Pascal does allow such a definition. It also allows many other standard functions to be called in defining the value of a constant.

In addition, Turbo Pascal provides another feature called *typed constants*. The definition of a typed constant specifies both a type and a value. This feature can be used to define constants that are arrays, records, sets, and several other more complicated data types.

case Statement in Turbo Pascal

In standard Pascal, the variable or expression used to select alternatives in a case statement must have one of the values listed in the case. If an unlisted value is encountered, the program will terminate with a run-time error. Thus it is necessary to use an if statement to guard the case, as described on p. 194 of your text.

This is not true in Turbo Pascal. An unlisted value does not cause a run-time error. Turbo Pascal allows an optional else clause to take care of values that are not listed in the case. If there is no else clause, the program simply continues with the next statement after the `case`. For example, lines 850-861 of the procedure `CheckCommand` (see Fig. 8.14) could be written in Turbo Pascal as

```
case Command.CommandCode of
   'Q'     : if (Command.Parameter1 = ' ')
             and (Command.Parameter2 = ' ')
             then CommandIsCorrect := true;
   'B','H' : if (Command.Parameter1 in ['a'..'z'])
             and (Command.Parameter2 = ' ')
             then CommandIsCorrect := true;
   'S'     : if (Command.Parameter1 in ['a'..'z'])
             and (Command.Parameter2 in ['A'..'Z'])
             then CommandIsCorrect := true;
   else
     { take some error correcting action }
   end   { case }
```

In most situations, the `else` clause would contain statements to take some appropriate action -- perhaps displaying an error message. In the actual procedure `CheckCommand`, there is no action to be taken if `Command.CommandCode` is not one of the listed values. Thus the `else` clause could be omitted.

Moving Procedures between Programs

As the text discusses, it is often desirable to reuse (or modify) previously written procedures and functions when writing a new program. For example, suppose that you are doing Programming Project 8.5. You might want to use the procedures `GetCipher`, `DisplayPlaintext`, and `Substitute` from the program Solve.

You can do this using the same techniques that we discussed in Exercise 5.4. When you want to reuse a procedure from the program Solve, select File I Open to open a new window that contains Solve. Highlight the procedure that you want to reuse, and select Edit I Copy to copy it to the clipboard. Then use Window I Next to switch back to the window that contains the program you are writing. Select Edit I Paste to paste the copied procedure into your new program. If you want to copy another procedure, you can switch back to the Solve window by selecting Window I Next again. When you have finished copying procedures from the program Solve, you can switch to the Solve window and select Window I Close to close it.

CHAPTER

9

Exercise 9.1

The program Index1 reads its input from a file named IDATA. Your directory CHAP9 contains a file named IDATA1 that you want to use as input for Index1. You can do this by changing the assign statement to read

```
assign(IDATA,'IDATA1');
```

If you prefer to avoid changing the program, you could simply create a file named IDATA by making a copy of IDATA1.

Specifying File Names at Run Time

The discussion of Exercise 9.1 shows how to supply the name of a file when compiling a program. It is also possible to specify a file name when the program runs. (This means that you would not have to recompile the program each time you want to use a different data file.) To do this, you make the file name in the assign statement a variable (a packed array of characters), not a quoted string. For example, the following code would allow Index1 to read the name of the data file at run time.

```
procedure Initialize(...);
var
  I : integer;
  FileName : packed array [1..12] of char;
  .
begin { Initialize }
  .
    write('Enter file name: ');
    for I := 1 to 12 do
      if eoln(input) then
        FileName[I] := ' '
      else
        read(FileName[I]);
    readln;
    assign(IDATA,FileName);
  .
end; { Initialize }
```

Strings in Turbo Pascal

In standard Pascal, you can compare two strings, or assign the value of one string to another, only if the two strings have the same length. For example, suppose that `TextWord` is defined as shown in Fig. 9.4 in your text:

```
const
  MaximumWordLength = 20;
  .
type
  AlphaString = packed array [1..MaximumWordLength] of char;
  .
var
  TextWord : AlphaString;
```

In this case, `TextWord` is 20 characters long. Thus to store the word *exercise* in the variable `TextWord`, we would have to write

```
TextWord := 'exercise
```

To test whether `TextWord` contains the word *the,* we would have to write

```
if TextWord = 'the                    ' then...
```

In Turbo Pascal, a string that is defined in this way (as a packed array of characters) is referred to as a *packed string*. There is also another data type, called simply `string`, that relaxes these restrictions. For example, in Turbo Pascal we could declare

```
var
  TextWord : string[20];
```

This defines `TextWord` as a string with maximum length 20 characters. When a value is assigned to a `string` variable, Turbo Pascal automatically keeps track of the actual number of characters in the string. Thus it is not necessary for strings being assigned or compared to have the same length. For example, if `TextWord` is declared with type `string`, the statements

```
TextWord := 'exercise';
```

and

```
if TextWord = 'the' then...
```

would be allowed.

Warning: If `TextWord` is declared as an ordinary Pascal-style string (a packed array of characters), a comparison like `(TextWord = 'the')` will not work properly. However, Turbo Pascal will not give you a compilation error -- you will have to find the problem yourself.

Turbo Pascal provides many different procedures and functions that perform operations on strings (both the type `string` and ordinary Pascal-style packed strings). You may want to read about some of these in the Turbo Pascal manual. However, you should be aware that these procedures and functions, and the type `string` itself, are non-standard. If you use these features, your program will probably not run with any compiler except Turbo Pascal.

Set Constants

As the text mentions (p. 211), standard Pascal does not allow set constants. However, many compilers do provide such a feature. In Turbo Pascal, you could define the set `LegalCharacters` (see Fig. 9.6) as a constant by writing

```
const
  Quote = '''';
  LegalCharacters = ['a'..'z',Quote];
```

Including Source Files

You can instruct Turbo Pascal to include another source file in your program by writing a comment of the form

```
{$I filename }
```

(This is the same method that is described on pages 219-220 of your text.) If no extension is specified in the filename, `.PAS` is assumed. If the file to be included is not in your current directory, you can specify a directory as part of the filename. (You can also accomplish this by entering an "include directory" in the Options | Directories dialog box.)

CHAPTER

10

Limitation on Set Size

In Turbo Pascal, a set can have no more than 256 potential members. Thus, for example,

```
set of 0..255
```

would be a legal type, but

```
set of 0..256
```

would be illegal.

Exercises 10.4 - 10.6

In these exercises, you are asked to compare the lengths of time that different versions of the indexing program take to run. Remember that the times you observe are actually a combination of several different factors -- the time your program takes to perform calculations, the time it takes to read and write data, and the time used by DOS and Turbo Pascal to manage the process.

Many systems have programming tools that let you do a better job of comparisons like these. For example, you might be able to measure exactly how much time your program takes to do computations, ignoring the time the computer spends doing other things. In a later course, you may use such tools to study the efficiency of different programs and algorithms.

CHAPTER

11

Exercise 11.1

Because of its size, the dictionary file WORDLIST is not stored in the directory CHAP11 that you copied to your program disk. Instead, you want the program Anagram1 to read this dictionary file from the hard disk of your computer. In order to accomplish this, you must tell the program where WORDLIST is located.

Your instructor will tell you the drive name of the hard disk and the directory name where WORDLIST is stored. Before you compile Anagram1, include this information in the assign statement for WORDLIST. For example, if the hard disk is drive C: and the directory name is \PROGRAMS\DICTION, you would change the assign statement to read

```
assign(WORDLIST,'C:\PROGRAMS\DICTION\WORDLIST');
```

You will need to do the same thing again later, when you compile and run Anagram2.

Detecting Subrange Errors

One of the advantages of using subrange types is the ability to detect values that are out of the proper range as soon as they occur. (See the discussion on pp. 308-309 in your text.) Turbo Pascal does not check for this error unless you request it. To request the checking of subrange values, select Options | Compiler and choose "Range checking" in the dialog box that appears.

Object-Oriented Programming

The programs that you studied in this chapter made use of an abstract data type named PhraseType. As you saw, it is possible to use PhraseType in a program without worrying about how phrases are represented and how operations on phrases are performed.

Turbo Pascal supports a methodology known as *object-oriented programming* that extends and improves on these original ideas of data abstraction. A data representation and the procedures and functions that manipulate it are combined to form a new data type called an *object*. Other objects can be defined as "descendants" of the original object. These descendants inherit access to all of the code and data defined by their ancestors. However, each descendant can also implement actions on the data being represented in a way that is appropriate to itself. This approach provides a high level of data abstraction, and can lead to the creation of programs that are more structured, more flexible, and easier to maintain.

You will learn more about object-oriented programming as you continue your study of computer science. If you want to find out more now, the Turbo Pascal manual has an excellent tutorial on the subject.

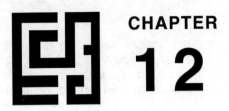

CHAPTER

12

Exercise 12.1

This exercise could take a long time to run completely. Remember that you can stop the program at any time by typing <Ctrl+Break>.

Exercise 12.2

The dictionary file WORDSORT is stored on the hard disk, in the same directory as WORDLIST. Change the assign statement for WORDSORT to include this information, in the same way you did in Exercise 11.1.

Exercise 12.3

The file DICTFILE that you will create in this exercise is very large -- in fact, it may be too large to fit on a diskette, even if no other files are present. Your instructor will tell you the name of a directory on the hard disk where you can create this file. Enter this name in the assign statement for DICTFILE. Remember also to supply the directory name for WORDSORT, as you did in Exercise 12.2.

After you have run the program MakeDict, you can look at the sizes of the files by using the command dir. Supply the full name (including the drive) for the directory that you want to list. For example, if the file WORDSORT is in the directory C:\PROGRAMS\DICTION, you would enter

```
dir c:\programs\diction
```

You should see a listing that looks like

```
Directory of C:\PROGRAMS\DICTION

WORDLIST      160471   3-09-94    1:06p
WORDSORT      160471   3-09-94    1:06p
```

The date and time tell you when the file was last modified. The number following the file name tells you the size of the file. Thus, this listing says that WORDLIST and WORDSORT are both 160,471 bytes long. (A byte is a unit of storage; for textfiles, one byte usually corresponds to one character.)

Follow the same procedure to list the directory containing DICTFILE. For example, if you created this file in the directory C:\PROGRAMS\TEMP, you would enter

```
dir c:\programs\temp
```

You will notice that DICTFILE is more than 8 times as long as WORDSORT.

Because DICTFILE is so large, you will probably want to delete it after you complete the exercises for this chapter. As usual, you can do this with the command erase. Be sure to supply the drive name and directory name -- for example

```
erase c:\programs\temp\dictfile
```

Exercise 12.4

In previous chapters, you have examined the contents of a file by using Turbo Pascal. Try this now by entering the command

```
turbo c:\programs\temp\dictfile.
```

As before, you will need to supply the drive name and directory name given to you by your instructor. Remember that you need to include the period so Turbo Pascal knows that you mean the file DICTFILE, not DICTFILE.PAS.

It may take a long time for Turbo Pascal to open this file, because it is so large. You may get an error message, and your screen will probably be filled with strange characters. This behavior occurs because Turbo Pascal is designed to work only with textfiles, and DICTFILE is not a textfile. A similar thing would happen if you accidentally tried to use Turbo Pascal on the executable version of a program that has already been compiled. (Such programs are usually stored in files with the extension .EXE.)

Direct Access Files

In standard Pascal, the only way to read a file is to start at the beginning. The data in the file must then be read in sequence, one element at a time. However, Turbo Pascal provides a Seek procedure that allows the program to go directly to a specified place in a typed file. (This operation cannot be used with textfiles.)

For example, suppose that a dictionary file contains 18,000 words. We could use Seek to go directly to word number 9,000 in the file. We could determine which half of the file contains the word we are looking for, and use Seek again to examine the word in the middle of that half. (In effect, we would be doing a binary search on the dictionary file.) Or we could use a separate index to determine the approximate position of the word in the file, and begin our search from there. (This would be similar to using the "thumb index" that is often cut into the pages of a dictionary in book form.)

Files that are designed to be accessed in this way are often referred to as *direct access* files.

CHAPTER

13

Controlling the Speed of the Display

On some computers, the program Life might run so fast that it is hard to see what is happening on the screen. To prevent this, the following statement has been inserted near the end of the procedure `Display`:

```
Delay(DelayCount);
```

This statement calls a non-standard Turbo Pascal procedure that delays the execution of the program for a specified number of milliseconds. The constant `DelayCount` (defined in the procedure `Display`) has the value 250; this corresponds to a delay of one-fourth of a second for each generation that is displayed. You may want to change this value if Life runs too fast or too slow on your computer.

Random Number Generating Routines

The random number generating routines in Turbo Pascal are the same as those described in the text (see pp. 355-358). The function `Random` generates a random number. It can be called with no parameters

```
RandomNumber := Random;
```

or with a parameter value of type `word` (that is, an integer between 0 and 65,535) -- for example

```
RandomInteger := Random(100);
```

In the first case (no parameters), the function `Random` returns a `real` value in the range $0 \leq$ `Random` < 1. In the second case, the function returns an integer between 0 and the value of the parameter. For example, `Random(100)` would return an integer in the range $0 \leq$ `Random` < 100.

An initial seed for the random number generator can be supplied by assigning a value to the variable `RandSeed`, which is of type `longint`. The procedure `Randomize` can be used to set `RandSeed` to a value that is different each time the program runs, as described in the text.

Graphics Routines

The output from the program Life (and all of the other programs in this book) consists of a series of characters displayed on the screen. Turbo Pascal also provides a powerful library of more than 50 different graphics routines. These routines can be used to draw lines and figures on the screen, to control the colors being displayed, and to perform many other operations. The Turbo Pascal manuals contain detailed information about how to use these features. If you are interested, you might want to try converting the program Life to use graphics output.

CHAPTER
14

Exercise 14.1

The program Wator that you run in this exercise performs the same simulations as the one you ran in Chapter 1. When it is compiled, the version in this chapter includes procedures from the files DISPLAY.I, RANDOM.I, RECLIST.I, and SCREEN.I. For simplicity, the version in Chapter 1 had all of these procedures combined into the file WATOR.PAS. When all of these procedures are included, the total length of the program Wator is approximately 1600 lines.

The procedure Display (stored in the file DISPLAY.I) contains the same call to Delay that is described in Chapter 13 of this manual. As before, you may want to change the value of the constant DelayCount if Wator runs too fast or too slow on your computer.

EXAMPLE PROGRAM

Loan1

```
1    program Loan1(input,output);
2
3    {-----------------------------------------------------------------------}
4    {  This program simulates the financing of a purchase over a            }
5    {  one-year period, with the payments being drawn from a savings        }
6    {  account.  Interest on savings is paid monthly.  The program          }
7    {  displays the amount of interest earned, payment made, new savings    }
8    {  balance, interest paid, and new loan balance for each month.  It     }
9    {  also calculates and displays the total amount of interest earned     }
10   {  on savings for the year, and the total amount of interest paid       }
11   {  (finance charges) for the year.                                      }
12   {                                                                       }
13   {  Input :   none                                                       }
14   {                 (The amount being financed, monthly payment, starting }
15   {                  balance in savings, and interest rate on savings are }
16   {                  given by constants in the program.)                  }
17   {                                                                       }
18   {  Output :  Listing of interest earned, payment made, new savings      }
19   {                 balance, interest paid, and new loan balance for each }
20   {                 month from 1 (first month of loan) to 12 (last month  }
21   {                 of loan).  Listing of total interest earned and total }
22   {                 interest paid over the period of the loan.            }
23   {-----------------------------------------------------------------------}
24
25   const
26     AmountFinanced = 3000;          { amount financed }
27     PaymentAmount = 263.05;         { amount of monthly payment }
28     StartingBalance = 3000;         { starting balance in savings account }
29     SavingsRate = 0.065;            { annual interest rate on savings }
30     LoanRate = 0.095;               { annual interest rate on loan }
31
32   var
33     Month : integer;                { current month number, starting at 1 }
34     SavingsBalance : real;          { current savings balance }
35     LoanBalance : real;             { current loan balance }
36     InterestEarned : real;          { interest earned for current month }
37     InterestPaid : real;            { interest paid for current month   }
38     TotalInterestEarned : real;     { total interest earned }
39     TotalInterestPaid : real;       { total interest paid }
40
41   {**********************************************************************}
42
43   procedure Initialize;
```

```
44
45      {------------------------------------------------------------------}
46      {  Initialize is called once at the beginning of the program.    }
47      {  It sets the savings balance and loan balance to their starting }
48      {  values, and initializes the totals to zero.                   }
49      {------------------------------------------------------------------}
50
51      begin  { Initialize }
52
53         { set starting balances }
54
55         SavingsBalance := StartingBalance;
56         LoanBalance := AmountFinanced;
57
58         { initialize totals to zero }
59
60         TotalInterestEarned := 0;
61         TotalInterestPaid := 0
62
63      end;   { Initialize }
64
65   {*******************************************************************}
66
67   procedure WriteHeadings;
68
69      {------------------------------------------------------------------}
70      {  WriteHeadings is called once at the beginning of the program. }
71      {  It writes the headings for the listing of monthly results.    }
72      {------------------------------------------------------------------}
73
74      begin  { WriteHeadings }
75
76         writeln;
77         writeln('       INTEREST            SAVINGS   INTEREST    LOAN ');
78         writeln('MONTH   EARNED   PAYMENT   BALANCE     PAID    BALANCE');
79         writeln
80
81      end;   { WriteHeadings }
82
83   {*******************************************************************}
84
85   procedure ComputeNewBalance;
86
87      {------------------------------------------------------------------}
88      {  ComputeNewBalance is called once for each month of the loan.  }
89      {  It computes the amount of interest earned and the amount of   }
90      {  interest paid for the current month.  The new savings balance }
91      {  and new loan balance are computed, reflecting the interest    }
92      {  earned, interest paid, and loan payment made.  The interest   }
93      {  earned and interest paid are added to the yearly totals.      }
94      {------------------------------------------------------------------}
95
96      begin  { ComputeNewBalance }
```

```
97
98           {  compute interest earned and interest paid for one month --
99              monthly interest is 1/12 of annual interest }
100
101          InterestEarned := SavingsBalance * (SavingsRate / 12);
102          InterestPaid := LoanBalance * (LoanRate / 12);
103
104          {  compute new savings and loan balances }
105
106          SavingsBalance := SavingsBalance + InterestEarned - PaymentAmount;
107          LoanBalance := LoanBalance + InterestPaid - PaymentAmount;
108
109          {  add interest earned and interest paid to totals }
110
111          TotalInterestEarned := TotalInterestEarned + InterestEarned;
112          TotalInterestPaid := TotalInterestPaid + InterestPaid
113
114      end;    { ComputeNewBalance }
115
116  {*******************************************************************}
117
118  procedure WriteBalance;
119
120      {-----------------------------------------------------------------}
121      {  WriteBalance is called once for each month of the loan.  It    }
122      {  displays the month number, interest earned, payment made,      }
123      {  new savings balance, interest paid, and new loan balance.      }
124      {-----------------------------------------------------------------}
125
126      begin   { WriteBalance }
127
128         writeln(Month:5, InterestEarned:11:2, PaymentAmount:11:2,
129                  SavingsBalance:11:2, InterestPaid:11:2, LoanBalance:11:2)
130
131      end;    { WriteBalance }
132
133  {*******************************************************************}
134
135  procedure WriteTotals;
136
137      {-----------------------------------------------------------------}
138      {  WriteTotals is called once at the end of the program.  It      }
139      {  displays the total amount of interest earned and the total     }
140      {  amount of interest paid for the term of the loan.              }
141      {-----------------------------------------------------------------}
142
143      begin   { WriteTotals }
144
145         writeln;
146         writeln('TOTAL INTEREST PAID   = ', TotalInterestPaid:8:2);
147         writeln('TOTAL INTEREST EARNED = ', TotalInterestEarned:8:2);
148         writeln
149
```

```
150      end;    { WriteTotals }
151
152    {**********************************************************}
153
154    procedure CleanUp;
155
156      {---------------------------------------------------------}
157      {  CleanUp is called once at the end of the program.  It waits for  }
158      {  the user to enter a carriage return before exiting the program.  }
159      {---------------------------------------------------------}
160
161      begin   { CleanUp }
162
163        write('Press return to exit program');
164        readln
165
166      end;   { CleanUp }
167
168    {**********************************************************}
169
170    begin   { main program }
171
172      { initialize variables and write headings }
173
174      Initialize;
175      WriteHeadings;
176
177      { compute and write balances for each month of the loan }
178
179      for Month := 1 to 12 do
180        begin
181          ComputeNewBalance;
182          WriteBalance
183        end;
184
185      { write totals and exit program }
186
187      WriteTotals;
188      CleanUp
189
190    end.
```

EXAMPLE PROGRAM
Loan2

```
 1    program Loan2(input,output);
 2
 3    {----------------------------------------------------------------------}
 4    { This program simulates the financing of a purchase over a         }
 5    { one-year period, with the payments being drawn from a savings     }
 6    { account.  Interest on savings is paid monthly.  The program       }
 7    { displays the amount of interest earned, payment made, new savings }
 8    { balance, interest paid, and new loan balance for each month.  It  }
 9    { also calculates and displays the total amount of interest earned  }
10    { on savings for the year, and the total amount of interest paid    }
11    { (finance charges) for the year.                                   }
12    {                                                                   }
13    { Input :   none                                                    }
14    {              (The amount being financed, monthly payment, starting }
15    {               balance in savings, and interest rate on savings are }
16    {               given by constants in the program.)                 }
17    {                                                                   }
18    { Output :  Listing of interest earned, payment made, new savings   }
19    {              balance, interest paid, and new loan balance for each }
20    {              month from 1 (first month of loan) to 12 (last month }
21    {              of loan).  Listing of total interest earned and total }
22    {              interest paid over the period of the loan.           }
23    {                                                                   }
24    { Modification history:                                             }
25    {              This program performs the same input, output, and    }
26    {              computations as the original version (program Loan1). }
27    {              However, it uses parameters to pass information to and }
28    {              from procedures, whereas the original program used    }
29    {              global variables for this purpose.                   }
30    {----------------------------------------------------------------------}
31
32    const
33       AmountFinanced = 3000;        { amount financed }
34       PaymentAmount = 263.05;       { amount of monthly payment }
35       StartingBalance = 3000;       { starting balance in savings account }
36       SavingsRate = 0.065;          { annual interest rate on savings }
37       LoanRate = 0.095;             { annual interest rate on loan }
38
39    var
40       Month : integer;              { current month number, starting at 1 }
41       SavingsBalance : real;        { current savings balance }
42       LoanBalance : real;           { current loan balance }
43       InterestEarned : real;        { interest earned for current month }
```

```
44      InterestPaid : real;          { interest paid for current month   }
45      TotalInterestEarned : real;   { total interest earned }
46      TotalInterestPaid : real;     { total interest paid }
47
48   {********************************************************************}
49
50   procedure Initialize(var SavingsBalance : real; var LoanBalance : real;
51                  var TotalInterestEarned : real; var TotalInterestPaid : real);
52
53      {-------------------------------------------------------------------}
54      {  Initialize is called once at the beginning of the program.       }
55      {  It sets the savings balance and loan balance to their starting   }
56      {  values, and initializes the totals to zero.                      }
57      {                                                                   }
58      {  Input parameters: None                                           }
59      {                                                                   }
60      {  Output parameters:                                               }
61      {     SavingsBalance - starting savings balance from constant       }
62      {                      StartingBalance                              }
63      {     LoanBalance - starting loan balance from constant             }
64      {                   AmountFinanced                                  }
65      {     TotalInterestEarned - zero                                    }
66      {     TotalInterestPaid - zero                                      }
67      {-------------------------------------------------------------------}
68
69      begin  { Initialize }
70
71         { set starting balances }
72
73         SavingsBalance := StartingBalance;
74         LoanBalance := AmountFinanced;
75
76         { initialize totals to zero }
77
78         TotalInterestEarned := 0;
79         TotalInterestPaid := 0
80
81      end;   { Initialize }
82
83   {********************************************************************}
84
85   procedure WriteHeadings;
86
87      {-------------------------------------------------------------------}
88      {  WriteHeadings is called once at the beginning of the program.    }
89      {  It writes the headings for the listing of monthly results.       }
90      {-------------------------------------------------------------------}
91
92      begin  { WriteHeadings }
93
94         writeln;
95         writeln('          INTEREST                  SAVINGS    INTEREST    LOAN  ');
96         writeln('MONTH      EARNED    PAYMENT    BALANCE      PAID     BALANCE');
```

```
 97          writeln
 98
 99      end;    { WriteHeadings }
100
101    {*******************************************************************}
102
103    procedure ComputeNewBalance(var SavingsBalance : real;
104                    var InterestEarned : real; var TotalInterestEarned : real;
105                    var LoanBalance : real; var InterestPaid : real;
106                    var TotalInterestPaid : real);
107
108      {-------------------------------------------------------------------}
109      {  ComputeNewBalance is called once for each month of the loan.    }
110      {  It computes the amount of interest earned and the amount of     }
111      {  interest paid for the current month.  The new savings balance   }
112      {  and new loan balance are computed, reflecting the interest      }
113      {  earned, interest paid, and loan payment made.  The interest     }
114      {  earned and interest paid are added to the yearly totals.        }
115      {                                                                  }
116      {  Input parameters:                                               }
117      {    SavingsBalance - savings balance at start of the current month}
118      {    Loan Balance - loan balance at start of the current month     }
119      {    TotalInterestEarned - total interest earned on savings prior  }
120      {                         to the current month                     }
121      {    TotalInterestPaid - total interest paid on loan prior to the  }
122      {                         current month                            }
123      {                                                                  }
124      {  Output parameters:                                              }
125      {    SavingsBalance - savings balance at end of the current month  }
126      {    InterestEarned - amount of interest earned on savings for the }
127      {                         current month                            }
128      {    TotalInterestEarned - total interest earned on savings        }
129      {                         including the current month              }
130      {    LoanBalance - loan balance at end of the current month        }
131      {    InterestPaid - amount of interest paid on loan for the        }
132      {                         current month                            }
133      {    TotalInterestPaid - total interest paid on the loan including  }
134      {                         the current month                        }
135      {-------------------------------------------------------------------}
136
137      begin   { ComputeNewBalance }
138
139         { compute interest earned and interest paid for one month --
140           monthly interest is 1/12 of annual interest }
141
142         InterestEarned := SavingsBalance * (SavingsRate / 12);
143         InterestPaid := LoanBalance * (LoanRate / 12);
144
145         { compute new savings and loan balances }
146
147         SavingsBalance := SavingsBalance + InterestEarned - PaymentAmount;
148         LoanBalance := LoanBalance + InterestPaid - PaymentAmount;
149
```

```
150          {  add interest earned and interest paid to totals }
151
152          TotalInterestEarned := TotalInterestEarned + InterestEarned;
153          TotalInterestPaid := TotalInterestPaid + InterestPaid
154
155      end;    { ComputeNewBalance }
156
157   {************************************************************}
158
159   procedure WriteBalance(Month : integer; SavingsBalance : real;
160               InterestEarned : real; LoanBalance : real; InterestPaid : real);
161
162      {-----------------------------------------------------------}
163      {  WriteBalance is called once for each month of the loan.  It    }
164      {  displays the month number, interest earned, payment made,      }
165      {  new savings balance, interest paid, and new loan balance.      }
166      {                                                                 }
167      {  Input parameters:                                              }
168      {    Month - current month number                                }
169      {    SavingsBalance - savings balance at end of the current month }
170      {    InterestEarned - interest earned on savings for current month }
171      {    LoanBalance - loan balance at end of the current month        }
172      {    InterestPaid - interest paid on loan for the current month    }
173      {                                                                 }
174      {  Output parameters : None                                       }
175      {-----------------------------------------------------------}
176
177      begin   { WriteBalance }
178
179         writeln(Month:5, InterestEarned:11:2, PaymentAmount:11:2,
180                 SavingsBalance:11:2, InterestPaid:11:2, LoanBalance:11:2)
181
182      end;    { WriteBalance }
183
184   {************************************************************}
185
186   procedure WriteTotals(TotalInterestEarned : real; TotalInterestPaid : real);
187
188      {-----------------------------------------------------------}
189      {  WriteTotals is called once at the end of the program.  It      }
190      {  displays the total amount of interest earned and the total     }
191      {  amount of interest paid for the term of the loan.              }
192      {                                                                 }
193      {  Input parameters:                                              }
194      {    TotalInterestEarned - total amount of interest earned on     }
195      {                          savings                                }
196      {    TotalInterestPaid - total amount of interest paid on the loan }
197      {                                                                 }
198      {  Output parameters: None                                        }
199      {-----------------------------------------------------------}
200
201      begin   { WriteTotals }
202
```

```
203        writeln;
204        writeln('TOTAL INTEREST PAID   = ', TotalInterestPaid:8:2);
205        writeln('TOTAL INTEREST EARNED = ', TotalInterestEarned:8:2);
206        writeln
207
208     end;   { WriteTotals }
209
210   {*******************************************************************}
211
212   procedure CleanUp;
213
214      {-----------------------------------------------------------------}
215      {  CleanUp is called once at the end of the program.  It waits for }
216      {  the user to enter a carriage return before exiting the program. }
217      {-----------------------------------------------------------------}
218
219      begin   { CleanUp }
220
221        write('Press return to exit program');
222        readln
223
224      end;   { CleanUp }
225
226   {*******************************************************************}
227
228   begin   { main program }
229
230      { initialize variables and write headings }
231
232      Initialize(SavingsBalance,LoanBalance,TotalInterestEarned,TotalInterestPaid);
233      WriteHeadings;
234
235      { compute and write balances for each month of the loan }
236
237      for Month := 1 to 12 do
238        begin
239          ComputeNewBalance(SavingsBalance,InterestEarned,TotalInterestEarned,
240                            LoanBalance,InterestPaid,TotalInterestPaid);
241          WriteBalance(Month,SavingsBalance,InterestEarned,LoanBalance,InterestPaid)
242        end;
243
244      { write totals and exit program }
245
246      WriteTotals(TotalInterestEarned,TotalInterestPaid);
247      CleanUp
248
249   end.
```

EXAMPLE PROGRAM
Loan3

```
1    program Loan3(input,output);
2
3    {-----------------------------------------------------------------------}
4    {  This program simulates the financing of a purchase, with the         }
5    {  with the payments being drawn from a savings account.  Interest      }
6    {  on savings is paid monthly.  The program displays the amount         }
7    {  of interest earned, payment made, new savings balance, interest      }
8    {  paid, and new loan balance for each month.  It continues to          }
9    {  compute and display results until the loan balance falls to zero.    }
10   {  At the end of the monthly listing, it displays the total amount      }
11   {  of interest earned on savings, and the total amount of interest      }
12   {  paid (finance charges).                                              }
13   {                                                                       }
14   {  Input :   The starting savings balance, interest rate on savings,    }
15   {            amount being financed, interest rate on the loan, and      }
16   {            amount of the monthly loan payment are entered from the    }
17   {            keyboard                                                    }
18   {                                                                       }
19   {  Output :  Listing of interest earned, payment made, new savings      }
20   {            balance, interest paid, and new loan balance for each      }
21   {            month.  Listing of total interest earned and total         }
22   {            interest paid over the period of the loan.                 }
23   {                                                                       }
24   {  Modification history:                                                }
25   {            This program performs the same monthly computations as     }
26   {            the previous version (Loan2).  However, the savings        }
27   {            balance is never allowed to become negative.  The          }
28   {            monthly listing continues until the loan balance falls     }
29   {            to zero.  The output listing pauses after each twelve      }
30   {            months, waiting for the user to enter a carriage return    }
31   {            before continuing.                                         }
32   {                                                                       }
33   {            The initial savings and loan balances, the interest        }
34   {            rates, and the monthly loan payment are entered by the     }
35   {            user, instead of being defined as constants in the         }
36   {            program.  The balances, interest rates, and other          }
37   {            information for the savings account and the loan           }
38   {            account are gathered together into records for clarity     }
39   {            and ease of parameter handling.                            }
40   {-----------------------------------------------------------------------}
41
42   type
43
```

```
44      SavingsAccount = record                    { savings account information }
45                      StartingBalance : real;    { starting balance }
46                      SavingsRate : real;        { interest rate }
47                      SavingsBalance : real;     { current balance }
48                      InterestEarned : real;     { interest earned this month }
49                      TotalInterestEarned : real { total interest to date }
50                  end;
51
52      LoanAccount = record                       { loan account information }
53                    AmountFinanced : real;       { starting loan amount }
54                    LoanRate : real;             { interest rate }
55                    RegularPayment : real;       { regular payment amount }
56                    CurrentPayment : real;       { current payment amount }
57                    LoanBalance : real;          { current balance }
58                    InterestPaid : real;         { interest paid this month }
59                    TotalInterestPaid : real     { total interest to date }
60                end;
61
62   var
63      Savings : SavingsAccount;     { savings account information }
64      Loan : LoanAccount;           { loan information }
65      Month : integer;              { current month number, starting at 1 }
66
67   {***********************************************************************}
68
69   procedure Initialize(var Savings : SavingsAccount; var Loan : LoanAccount);
70
71      {----------------------------------------------------------------}
72      {  Initialize is called once at the beginning of the program.    }
73      {  It prompts the user to enter starting savings and interest rates }
74      {  and interest rates, and the amount of the monthly loan payment. }
75      {  The values entered are stored in the records that represent the }
76      {  savings and loan accounts, and the totals are initialized to   }
77      {  zero.                                                          }
78      {                                                                 }
79      {  Input parameters: None                                        }
80      {                                                                 }
81      {  Output parameters:                                            }
82      {    Savings - savings account information at start of loan      }
83      {    Loan - loan account information at start of loan            }
84      {----------------------------------------------------------------}
85
86   begin  { Initialize }
87
88      { get starting savings balance }
89
90      write('Starting savings balance    : ');
91      readln(Savings.StartingBalance);
92
93      { get savings interest rate, converting percentage to decimal fraction }
94
95      write('Interest rate on savings (%) : ');
96      readln(Savings.SavingsRate);
```

```
97       Savings.SavingsRate := Savings.SavingsRate / 100;
98
99       { get starting loan amount }
100
101      write('Amount financed on loan        : ');
102      readln(Loan.AmountFinanced);
103
104      { get loan interest rate, converting percentage to decimal fraction }
105
106      write('Interest rate on loan (%)      : ');
107      readln(Loan.LoanRate);
108      Loan.LoanRate := Loan.LoanRate / 100;
109
110      { get amount of monthly loan payment }
111
112      write('Monthly payment on loan        : ');
113      readln(Loan.RegularPayment);
114
115      { set starting balances for savings account and loan }
116
117      Savings.SavingsBalance := Savings.StartingBalance;
118      Loan.LoanBalance := Loan.AmountFinanced;
119
120      { initialize totals to zero }
121
122      Savings.TotalInterestEarned := 0;
123      Loan.TotalInterestPaid := 0
124
125    end;    { Initialize }
126
127  {*********************************************************************}
128
129  procedure WriteHeadings;
130
131    {-------------------------------------------------------------------}
132    {  WriteHeadings is called once at the beginning of the program.    }
133    {  It writes the headings for the listing of monthly results.       }
134    {-------------------------------------------------------------------}
135
136    begin   { WriteHeadings }
137
138      writeln;
139      writeln('          INTEREST               SAVINGS     INTEREST     LOAN  ');
140      writeln('MONTH     EARNED     PAYMENT     BALANCE      PAID     BALANCE');
141      writeln
142
143    end;    { WriteHeadings }
144
145  {*********************************************************************}
146
147  procedure ComputeNewBalance(var Savings : SavingsAccount;
148                              var Loan : LoanAccount);
149
```

```
150     {------------------------------------------------------------------}
151     {  ComputeNewBalance is called once for each month of the loan.    }
152     {  It computes the amount of interest earned and the amount of     }
153     {  interest paid for the current month.  The new savings balance   }
154     {  and new loan balance are computed, reflecting the interest      }
155     {  earned, interest paid, and loan payment made.  The interest     }
156     {  earned and interest paid are added to the totals.               }
157     {                                                                  }
158     {  Input parameters:                                               }
159     {    Savings - savings account information at start of the         }
160     {                 current month                                    }
161     {    Loan - loan account information at start of the current month }
162     {                                                                  }
163     {  Output parameters:                                              }
164     {    Savings - savings account information at end of current month }
165     {    Loan - loan account information at end of the current month   }
166     {------------------------------------------------------------------}
167
168     begin  { ComputeNewBalance }
169
170        {  compute interest earned and interest paid for one month --
171            monthly interest is 1/12 of annual interest }
172
173        Savings.InterestEarned :=
174                        Savings.SavingsBalance * (Savings.SavingsRate / 12);
175        Loan.InterestPaid := Loan.LoanBalance * (Loan.LoanRate / 12);
176
177        {  compute amount owed on the loan, including interest }
178
179        Loan.LoanBalance := Loan.LoanBalance + Loan.InterestPaid;
180
181        {  set the current payment equal to the regular payment or the amount
182            owed, whichever is smaller }
183
184        if Loan.LoanBalance > Loan.RegularPayment then
185          Loan.CurrentPayment := Loan.RegularPayment
186        else
187          Loan.CurrentPayment := Loan.LoanBalance;
188
189        {  subtract the current payment to find the new loan balance }
190
191        Loan.LoanBalance := Loan.LoanBalance - Loan.CurrentPayment;
192
193        {  compute new savings balance }
194
195        Savings.SavingsBalance := Savings.SavingsBalance
196                            + Savings.InterestEarned - Loan.CurrentPayment;
197
198        {  if the savings balance would become negative, set it to zero }
199
200        if Savings.SavingsBalance < 0 then
201          Savings.SavingsBalance := 0;
202
```

```
203        {  add interest earned and interest paid to totals }
204
205        Savings.TotalInterestEarned := Savings.TotalInterestEarned
206                                    + Savings.InterestEarned;
207        Loan.TotalInterestPaid := Loan.TotalInterestPaid + Loan.InterestPaid
208
209     end;    { ComputeNewBalance }
210
211   {*********************************************************************}
212
213   procedure WriteBalance(Month : integer; Savings : SavingsAccount;
214                          Loan : LoanAccount);
215
216      {-------------------------------------------------------------------}
217      {  WriteBalance is called once for each month of the loan.  It      }
218      {  displays the month number, interest earned, payment made,        }
219      {  new savings balance, interest paid, and new loan balance.        }
220      {                                                                   }
221      {  Input parameters:                                                }
222      {    Month - current month number                                   }
223      {    Savings - savings account information at end of current month  }
224      {    Loan - loan account information at end of the current month    }
225      {                                                                   }
226      {  Output parameters : None                                         }
227      {-------------------------------------------------------------------}
228
229      begin  { WriteBalance }
230
231         { write savings and loan information for current month }
232
233         writeln(Month:5, Savings.InterestEarned:11:2, Loan.CurrentPayment:11:2,
234                 Savings.SavingsBalance:11:2, Loan.InterestPaid:11:2,
235                 Loan.LoanBalance:11:2);
236
237         { if current month is a multiple of 12, wait until the user enters
238           a carriage return before continuing }
239
240         if (Month mod 12) = 0 then
241           begin
242             writeln;
243             write('Press return to continue');
244             readln
245           end
246
247      end;   { WriteBalance }
248
249   {*********************************************************************}
250
251   procedure WriteTotals(Savings : SavingsAccount; Loan : LoanAccount);
252
253      {-------------------------------------------------------------------}
254      {  WriteTotals is called once at the end of the program.  It        }
255      {  displays the total amount of interest earned and the total       }
```

```
256      {   amount of interest paid for the months covered in the listing.   }
257      {                                                                     }
258      {   Input parameters:                                                 }
259      {     Savings - savings account information at end of final month     }
260      {     Loan - loan account information at end of final month           }
261      {                                                                     }
262      {   Output parameters: None                                          }
263      {---------------------------------------------------------------------}
264
265      begin   { WriteTotals }
266
267        writeln;
268        writeln('TOTAL INTEREST PAID   = ', Loan.TotalInterestPaid:8:2);
269        writeln('TOTAL INTEREST EARNED = ', Savings.TotalInterestEarned:8:2);
270        writeln
271
272      end;    { WriteTotals }
273
274      {*********************************************************************}
275
276      procedure CleanUp;
277
278        {-------------------------------------------------------------------}
279        {  CleanUp is called once at the end of the program.  It waits for  }
280        {  the user to enter a carriage return before exiting the program.  }
281        {-------------------------------------------------------------------}
282
283      begin   { CleanUp }
284
285        write('Press return to exit program');
286        readln
287
288      end;   { CleanUp }
289
290      {*********************************************************************}
291
292      begin   { main program }
293
294        { initialize variables and write headings }
295
296        Initialize(Savings,Loan);
297        WriteHeadings;
298
299        { compute and write balances for each month of the loan }
300
301        Month := 0;
302        while Loan.LoanBalance > 0 do
303          begin
304            Month := Month + 1;
305            ComputeNewBalance(Savings,Loan);
306            WriteBalance(Month,Savings,Loan)
307          end;
308
```

```
309      { write totals and exit program }
310
311      WriteTotals(Savings,Loan);
312      CleanUp
313
314    end.
```

EXAMPLE PROGRAM
Cipher

```
1    program Cipher(input,output,KEYS);
2
3    {----------------------------------------------------------------------}
4    {  This program enciphers and deciphers messages using a simple        }
5    {  substitution cipher.  Messages are entered from the keyboard,       }
6    {  along with a command code requesting that they be enciphered  or    }
7    {  deciphered.  The keys used for enciphering and deciphering are      }
8    {  read from file KEYS.  The result of the requested enciphering or    }
9    {  deciphering is written back to the terminal.                        }
10   {                                                                      }
11   {  The user is prompted for each command to be entered.  The possible  }
12   {  commands are                                                        }
13   {          E - encipher the following message                          }
14   {          D - decipher the following message                          }
15   {          Q - quit execution of the program                           }
16   {  If the command entered is E or D, the user is then prompted to      }
17   {  enter the message to be enciphered or deciphered.                   }
18   {                                                                      }
19   {  Commands and messages may be entered using any combination of       }
20   {  upper case and lower case letters.  The output messages produced    }
21   {  by the program are in upper case for deciphered messages and lower  }
22   {  case for enciphered messages.  Non-alphabetic characters may be     }
23   {  included in messages, and are reproduced in the enciphered or       }
24   {  deciphered message without change.                                  }
25   {                                                                      }
26   {  The enciphering and deciphering keys are stored in file KEYS in     }
27   {  two lines.  The first line gives the encipherment for each          }
28   {  (plaintext) letter 'a' through 'z', in lower case.  The second      }
29   {  line gives the decipherment of each (ciphertext) letter             }
30   {  'a' through 'z', in upper case.  The enciphering key should         }
31   {  contain only lower case characters, and the deciphering key should  }
32   {  contain only upper case characters.  For example, the enciphering   }
33   {  key might be                                                        }
34   {                    owbsyfdahnegpqiurtljkmzxcv                        }
35   {  and the corresponding deciphering key might be                      }
36   {                    HCYGKFLIOTUSVJAMNQDRPZBXEW                        }
37   {                                                                      }
38   {  Input:  Commands and messages as described above, entered from the  }
39   {          terminal.  Enciphering and deciphering keys, read from      }
40   {          file KEYS.                                                  }
41   {                                                                      }
42   {  Output: Enciphered and deciphered messages, displayed on the        }
43   {          terminal.                                                   }
```

```
44   {                                                                      }
45   {  This program contains non-standard Pascal statements to support     }
46   {  Turbo Pascal and Berkeley Pascal versions.  Non-standard Pascal     }
47   {  statements appear in the following locations:                       }
48   {     1. in procedures Initialize and CleanUp                          }
49   {  These non-standard statements are preceded by a comment that        }
50   {  begins with '## N'.                                                 }
51   {----------------------------------------------------------------------}
52
53   const
54     MaximumLength = 80;              { maximum length of message to be processed }
55
56   type
57     Message = array[1..MaximumLength] of char;
58     Key = array['a'..'z'] of char;
59
60   var
61     KEYS : text;                    { file containing keys }
62     EncipherKey : Key;              { enciphering key }
63     DecipherKey : Key;              { deciphering key }
64     Command : char;                 { command entered from terminal }
65     Plaintext : Message;            { message to be enciphered }
66     Ciphertext : Message;           { message to be deciphered }
67     MessageLength : integer;        { length of message being processed }
68
69   {********************************************************************}
70
71   function Lowercase(Letter : char) : char;
72
73     {----------------------------------------------------------------}
74     {  Lowercase is used to convert alphabetic characters to lower    }
75     {  case.  If the input parameter is an upper case letter          }
76     {  ('A' through 'Z'), the value of the function is the corresponding}
77     {  lower case letter ('a' through 'z').  If the input parameter is }
78     {  any other character, the value of the function is equal to the  }
79     {  input parameter.                                               }
80     {                                                                 }
81     {  Input parameters:                                              }
82     {    Letter - character to be converted to lower case             }
83     {                                                                 }
84     {  Output parameters : None                                       }
85     {                                                                 }
86     {  Function value : the value of the input parameter Letter,      }
87     {                   converted to lower case if it was originally  }
88     {                   in the range 'A' through 'Z'                  }
89     {----------------------------------------------------------------}
90
91     var
92       ConvertedLetter : char;         { the function value being computed }
93       DistancePastA : integer;        { the distance in the alphabet between
94                                          the letter being converted and 'A' }
95     begin  { Lowercase }
96
```

```
 97            { if the input parameter is an upper case letter, convert it to
 98               the corresponding lower case letter.  otherwise, the converted
 99               letter is set equal to the input parameter. }
100
101            if (Letter >= 'A') and (Letter <= 'Z') then
102              begin
103                DistancePastA := ord(Letter) - ord('A');
104                ConvertedLetter := chr(ord('a') + DistancePastA)
105              end  { if }
106            else
107              ConvertedLetter := Letter;
108
109            { set the function value }
110
111            Lowercase := ConvertedLetter
112
113        end;  { Lowercase }
114
115   {********************************************************************}
116
117   function Uppercase(Letter : char) : char;
118
119      {-------------------------------------------------------------------}
120      {  Uppercase is used to convert alphabetic characters to upper     }
121      {  case.  If the input parameter is a lower case letter            }
122      {  ('a' through 'z'), the value of the function is the corresponding}
123      {  upper case letter ('A' through 'Z').  If the input parameter is  }
124      {  any other character, the value of the function is equal to the   }
125      {  input parameter.                                                 }
126      {                                                                   }
127      {  Input parameters:                                                }
128      {    Letter - character to be converted to upper case               }
129      {                                                                   }
130      {  Output parameters : None                                         }
131      {                                                                   }
132      {  Function value : the value of the input parameter Letter,        }
133      {                   converted to upper case if it was originally    }
134      {                   in the range 'a' through 'z'                    }
135      {-------------------------------------------------------------------}
136
137      var
138        ConvertedLetter : char;      { the function value being computed }
139        DistancePastA : integer;     { the distance in the alphabet between
140                                       the letter being converted and 'a' }
141      begin  { Uppercase }
142
143        { if the input parameter is a lower case letter, convert it to
144          the corresponding upper case letter.  otherwise, the converted
145          letter is set equal to the input parameter. }
146
147        if (Letter >= 'a') and (Letter <= 'z') then
148          begin
149            DistancePastA := ord(Letter) - ord('a');
```

```
150            ConvertedLetter := chr(ord('A') + DistancePastA)
151          end   { if }
152        else
153          ConvertedLetter := Letter;
154
155      { set the function value }
156
157      Uppercase := ConvertedLetter
158
159    end;   { Uppercase }
160
161  {*******************************************************************}
162
163  procedure Initialize;
164
165      {----------------------------------------------------------------}
166      {   Initialize is called once at the beginning of the program.   It   }
167      {   opens the input file KEYS.                                         }
168      {----------------------------------------------------------------}
169
170    begin   { Initialize }
171
172       { ## Non-standard statements -- Turbo Pascal version }
173
174       assign(KEYS,'KEYS');
175
176       { End Turbo Pascal version }
177
178       reset(KEYS);
179
180    end;   { Initialize }
181
182  {*******************************************************************}
183
184  procedure GetKeys(var EncipherKey,DecipherKey : Key);
185
186      {----------------------------------------------------------------}
187      {   GetKeys is called once.  It reads the file KEYS and stores the   }
188      {   enciphering and deciphering keys for later use.  Notice that     }
189      {   both enciphering and deciphering keys are stored in arrays        }
190      {   with subscripts ranging from 'a' to 'z'.                          }
191      {                                                                     }
192      {   Input parameters: None                                           }
193      {                                                                     }
194      {   Output parameters:                                               }
195      {     EncipherKey - the enciphering key to be used                    }
196      {     DecipherKey - the deciphering key to be used                    }
197      {----------------------------------------------------------------}
198
199    var
200       Letter : char;    { used as a subscript for EncipherKey and DecipherKey }
201
202    begin
```

```
203
204          { read enciphering and deciphering keys }
205
206          for Letter := 'a' to 'z' do
207            read(KEYS,EncipherKey[Letter]);
208
209          readln(KEYS);
210
211          for Letter := 'a' to 'z' do
212            read(KEYS,DecipherKey[Letter]);
213
214          readln(KEYS)
215
216       end;  { GetKeys }
217
218    {*******************************************************************}
219
220    procedure GetCommand(var Command : char);
221
222       {-------------------------------------------------------------------}
223       {  GetCommand is called each time a command is to be read from the  }
224       {  terminal.  It prompts the user to enter a command, then reads    }
225       {  a character from the terminal and converts it to upper case.     }
226       {  The converted character is returned in the parameter Command.    }
227       {                                                                   }
228       {  Input parameters: None                                          }
229       {                                                                   }
230       {  Output parameters:                                              }
231       {     Command - the command character read, converted to upper case }
232       {-------------------------------------------------------------------}
233
234       var
235         Letter : char;     { command letter read from the terminal }
236
237       begin  { GetCommand }
238
239         write('Enter command (E,D,Q) : ');
240         readln(Letter);
241         Command := Uppercase(Letter)
242
243       end;  { GetCommand }
244
245    {*******************************************************************}
246
247    procedure ReadMessage(var InputMessage : Message; var MessageLength : integer);
248
249       {-------------------------------------------------------------------}
250       {  ReadMessage is called whenever the command entered was E or D.   }
251       {  It prompts the user to enter a message to be enciphered or        }
252       {  deciphered, and then reads this message from the terminal.  The  }
253       {  message read is returned in the parameter InputMessage, and its  }
254       {  length is returned in parameter MessageLength.  If the message    }
255       {  entered is shorter than MaximumLength, the rest of InputMessage   }
```

```
256    {  is filled with blanks.  If the message is longer than the      }
257    {  maximum length allowed, the excess characters are ignored and a }
258    {  warning message is displayed on the terminal.                   }
259    {                                                                  }
260    {  Input parameters: None                                          }
261    {                                                                  }
262    {  Output parameters:                                              }
263    {    Message - the message read from the terminal                  }
264    {    MessageLength - the length of the message read                }
265    {------------------------------------------------------------------}
266
267    var
268       CharacterCount : integer;          { number of characters read so far }
269       I : integer;                       { used as a subscript for InputMessage }
270
271    begin
272
273       { prompt user for input }
274
275       writeln('Enter message:');
276       CharacterCount := 0;
277
278       { read characters from the terminal until end-of-line is detected,
279         or the maximum size message has been read }
280
281       while (not eoln(input)) and (CharacterCount < MaximumLength) do
282         begin
283           CharacterCount := CharacterCount + 1;
284           read(InputMessage[CharacterCount])
285         end;
286
287       { fill unused elements in InputMessage with blanks }
288
289       for I := CharacterCount + 1 to MaximumLength do
290         InputMessage[I] := ' ';
291
292       { if end-of-line was detected, the message was of a proper length.
293         otherwise, the message was too long -- issue a warning to the user. }
294
295       if not eoln(input) then
296           writeln('*** Message truncated to maximum length of ',
297                   MaximumLength:3,' characters.');
298
299       { skip the end-of-line marker and any input remaining on the current line }
300
301       readln;
302
303       { set the message length }
304
305       MessageLength := CharacterCount
306
307    end;   { ReadMessage }
308
```

```
309   {**********************************************************************}
310
311   procedure ApplyCode(Original : Message; MessageLength : integer;
312                       KeyToUse : Key; var Transformed : Message);
313
314     {---------------------------------------------------------------------}
315     {  ApplyCode is called whenever a message is to be enciphered or    }
316     {  deciphered.  The message given in the parameter Original is      }
317     {  transformed by applying the (enciphering or deciphering) key     }
318     {  given in KeyToUse.  The result is returned in the parameter      }
319     {  Transformed.  The length of the message being processed is given }
320     {  by MessageLength.                                                }
321     {                                                                   }
322     {  Input parameters:                                                }
323     {    Original - the message to be enciphered or deciphered          }
324     {    MessageLength - the length of the message                      }
325     {    KeyToUse - the enciphering or deciphering key to be applied    }
326     {               to Original                                         }
327     {                                                                   }
328     {  Output parameters:                                               }
329     {    Transformed - the enciphered or deciphered message that        }
330     {                  results from applying KeyToUse to Original       }
331     {---------------------------------------------------------------------}
332
333     var
334       I : integer;          { used as subscript for Original and Transformed }
335       Character : char;      { character being enciphered or deciphered }
336
337     begin  { ApplyCode }
338
339       for I := 1 to MessageLength do
340         begin
341
342           { convert upper case character to lower case }
343
344           Character := Lowercase(Original[I]);
345
346           { if character is alphabetic, transform it according to the key;
347             otherwise, copy the character without change }
348
349           if (Character >= 'a') and (Character <= 'z') then
350             Transformed[I] := KeyToUse[Character]
351           else
352             Transformed[I] := Character
353         end  { for }
354
355     end;  { ApplyCode }
356
357   {**********************************************************************}
358
359   procedure WriteMessage(OutputMessage : Message; MessageLength : integer);
360
361     {---------------------------------------------------------------------}
```

```
362     {  WriteMessage is called whenever an enciphered or deciphered   }
363     {  message is to be written back to the terminal.                }
364     {                                                                }
365     {  Input parameters:                                             }
366     {     OutputMessage - the message to be displayed                }
367     {     MessageLength - the length of the message                  }
368     {                                                                }
369     {  Output parameters: None                                       }
370     {----------------------------------------------------------------}
371
372     var
373       I : integer;           { used as subscript for OutputMessage }
374
375     begin  { WriteMessage }
376
377       for I := 1 to MessageLength do
378         write(OutputMessage[I]);
379       writeln
380
381     end;  { WriteMessage }
382
383   {*****************************************************************}
384
385   procedure CleanUp;
386
387     {----------------------------------------------------------------}
388     {  CleanUp is called once at the end of the program.  It closes   }
389     {  the file KEYS, if this is required in the Pascal version being }
390     {  used.                                                          }
391     {----------------------------------------------------------------}
392
393     begin  { CleanUp }
394
395       { ## Non-standard statements -- Turbo Pascal version }
396
397       close(KEYS)
398
399       { End Turbo Pascal version }
400
401     end;  { CleanUp }
402
403   {*****************************************************************}
404
405   begin  { main program }
406
407     Initialize;
408
409     { read enciphering and deciphering keys and get first command }
410
411     GetKeys(EncipherKey,DecipherKey);
412     GetCommand(Command);
413
414     { read and process commands until command Q is entered }
```

```
415
416        while Command <> 'Q' do
417          begin
418            if Command = 'E' then
419              begin
420
421                { read message, encipher it, and write enciphered version }
422
423                ReadMessage(Plaintext,MessageLength);
424                ApplyCode(Plaintext,MessageLength,EncipherKey,Ciphertext);
425                WriteMessage(Ciphertext,MessageLength)
426              end   { if command was E }
427            else if Command = 'D' then
428              begin
429
430                { read message, decipher it, and write deciphered version }
431
432                ReadMessage(Ciphertext,MessageLength);
433                ApplyCode(Ciphertext,MessageLength,DecipherKey,Plaintext);
434                WriteMessage(Plaintext,MessageLength)
435              end   { if command was D }
436            else
437
438                { command was not a valid choice -- write error message }
439
440                writeln('Commands are E(ncipher), D(ecipher), Q(uit)');
441
442            { get the next command }
443
444            GetCommand(Command)
445          end;   { while command not Q }
446
447        { exit program }
448
449        CleanUp
450
451      end.
```

EXAMPLE PROGRAM
MakeKeys

```
1    program MakeKeys(input,output,KEYS);
2
3    {-----------------------------------------------------------------------}
4    {  This program creates a file named KEYS that contains enciphering  }
5    {  and deciphering keys for use by the program Cipher.  The first    }
6    {  line of the file contains the enciphering key, and the second     }
7    {  line contains the deciphering key.                                }
8    {                                                                    }
9    {  To generate these keys, the user is first prompted to enter a     }
10   {  string of letters from the terminal.  An enciphering key is       }
11   {  generated by taking these letters in the order they were entered  }
12   {  (with duplicate letters eliminated), followed by the letters      }
13   {  of the alphabet that do not appear in the string (in reverse      }
14   {  alphabetical order).  This sequence of letters gives the          }
15   {  encipherment for each (plaintext) letter 'a' through 'z', in      }
16   {  lower case.  The case of the letters entered by the user is not   }
17   {  significant.                                                      }
18   {                                                                    }
19   {  The deciphering key gives the decipherment of each (ciphertext)   }
20   {  letter 'a' through 'z', in upper case.  This key is generated to  }
21   {  be the inverse of the enciphering key.                            }
22   {                                                                    }
23   {  For example, if the user entered the string                      }
24   {          Communications of the ACM                                }
25   {  the enciphering key would be                                     }
26   {          comuniatsfhezyxwvrqplkjgdb                               }
27   {  and the deciphering key would be                                 }
28   {          GZAYLJXKFWVUCEBTSRIHDQPONM                               }
29   {                                                                    }
30   {  Input:  A string of up to 80 letters entered by the user.        }
31   {                                                                    }
32   {  Output: Enciphering and deciphering keys in the file KEYS,        }
33   {          generated as described above.  These keys are also       }
34   {          displayed on the terminal.                               }
35   {                                                                    }
36   {  This program contains non-standard Pascal statements to support  }
37   {  Turbo Pascal and Berkeley Pascal versions.  Non-standard Pascal   }
38   {  statements appear in the following locations:                     }
39   {    1. in procedures Initialize and CleanUp                         }
40   {  These non-standard statements are preceded by a comment that      }
41   {  begins with '## N'.                                               }
42   {-----------------------------------------------------------------------}
43
```

```
44    type
45      Key = array['a'..'z'] of char;          { encipherment or decipherment of the
46                                                 characters 'a' through 'z' }
47      KeyString = array[1..80] of char;
48
49    var
50      KEYS : text;                             { file to receive keys }
51      EncipherKey : Key;                       { enciphering key }
52      DecipherKey : Key;                       { deciphering key }
53      InputString : KeyString;                 { string entered by the user }
54      StringLength : integer;                  { length of InputString }
55
56    {**********************************************************************}
57
58    function Lowercase(Letter : char) : char;
59
60      {-------------------------------------------------------------------}
61      {  Lowercase is used to convert alphabetic characters to lower      }
62      {  case.  If the input parameter is an upper case letter            }
63      {  ('A' through 'Z'), the value of the function is the corresponding}
64      {  lower case letter ('a' through 'z').  If the input parameter is  }
65      {  any other character, the value of the function is equal to the   }
66      {  input parameter.                                                 }
67      {                                                                   }
68      {  Input parameters:                                                }
69      {     Letter - character to be converted to lower case              }
70      {                                                                   }
71      {  Output parameters : None                                         }
72      {                                                                   }
73      {  Function value : the value of the input parameter Letter,        }
74      {                   converted to lower case if it was originally    }
75      {                   in the range 'A' through 'Z'                    }
76      {-------------------------------------------------------------------}
77
78      var
79         ConvertedLetter : char;        { the function value being computed }
80         DistancePastA : integer;       { the distance in the alphabet between
81                                          the letter being converted and 'A' }
82      begin   { Lowercase }
83
84         { if the input parameter is an upper case letter, convert it to
85           the corresponding lower case letter.  otherwise, the converted
86           letter is set equal to the input parameter. }
87
88         if (Letter >= 'A') and (Letter <= 'Z') then
89           begin
90             DistancePastA := ord(Letter) - ord('A');
91             ConvertedLetter := chr(ord('a') + DistancePastA)
92           end   { if }
93         else
94           ConvertedLetter := Letter;
95
96         { set the function value }
```

```pascal
 97
 98          Lowercase := ConvertedLetter
 99
100       end;   { Lowercase }
101
102    {******************************************************************}
103
104    function Uppercase(Letter : char) : char;
105
106       {------------------------------------------------------------------}
107       { Uppercase is used to convert alphabetic characters to upper      }
108       { case.  If the input parameter is a lower case letter             }
109       { ('a' through 'z'), the value of the function is the corresponding}
110       { upper case letter ('A' through 'Z').  If the input parameter is  }
111       { any other character, the value of the function is equal to the   }
112       { input parameter.                                                 }
113       {                                                                  }
114       { Input parameters:                                                }
115       {    Letter - character to be converted to upper case              }
116       {                                                                  }
117       { Output parameters : None                                         }
118       {                                                                  }
119       { Function value : the value of the input parameter Letter,        }
120       {                  converted to upper case if it was originally    }
121       {                  in the range 'a' through 'z'                    }
122       {------------------------------------------------------------------}
123
124       var
125          ConvertedLetter : char;        { the function value being computed }
126          DistancePastA : integer;       { the distance in the alphabet between
127                                           the letter being converted and 'a' }
128       begin  { Uppercase }
129
130          { if the input parameter is a lower case letter, convert it to
131            the corresponding upper case letter.  otherwise, the converted
132            letter is set equal to the input parameter. }
133
134          if (Letter >= 'a') and (Letter <= 'z') then
135            begin
136              DistancePastA := ord(Letter) - ord('a');
137              ConvertedLetter := chr(ord('A') + DistancePastA)
138            end   { if }
139          else
140            ConvertedLetter := Letter;
141
142          { set the function value }
143
144          Uppercase := ConvertedLetter
145
146       end;   { Uppercase }
147
148    {******************************************************************}
149
```

```
150    procedure Initialize;
151
152       {---------------------------------------------------------------------}
153       {  Initialize is called once at the beginning of the program.         }
154       {  It opens the output file KEYS.                                     }
155       {---------------------------------------------------------------------}
156
157       begin  { Initialize }
158
159          { ## Non-standard statements -- Turbo Pascal version }
160
161          assign(KEYS,'KEYS');
162
163          { End Turbo Pascal version }
164
165          rewrite(KEYS)
166
167       end;  { Initialize }
168
169    {*********************************************************************}
170
171    procedure GetString(var InputString : KeyString; var StringLength : integer);
172
173       {---------------------------------------------------------------------}
174       {  GetString is called to obtain the input string from the user.      }
175       {  It prompts the user to enter a string of letters, then reads       }
176       {  the string from the terminal (a maximum of 80 letters).            }
177       {  Letters read are converted to lower case, and non-alphabetic       }
178       {  characters are discarded.  If more than 80 letters are entered,    }
179       {  the excess characters are skipped with no error message.           }
180       {                                                                     }
181       {  Input parameters: None                                            }
182       {                                                                     }
183       {  Output parameters:                                                }
184       {    InputString - the string of characters read from the terminal,  }
185       {                  with letters converted to lower case and          }
186       {                  non-alphabetic characters discarded.              }
187       {    StringLength - the number of letters in InputString             }
188       {---------------------------------------------------------------------}
189
190       var
191          CharacterCount : integer;     { number of characters placed in InputString }
192          Letter : char;                { character read from terminal }
193          ConvertedLetter : char;       { Letter converted to lower case }
194
195       begin  { GetString }
196
197          { prompt the user to enter a string of letters }
198
199          writeln('Enter key string (1 to 80 characters): ');
200          CharacterCount := 0;
201
202          { read and process letters until end-of-line is reached, or until
```

```
203        80 letters have been read }
204
205      while (not eoln(input)) and (CharacterCount < 80) do
206        begin
207
208          { read a character and convert it to lower case }
209
210          read(Letter);
211          ConvertedLetter := Lowercase(Letter);
212
213          { if the character read is alphabetic, add it to InputString }
214
215          if (ConvertedLetter >= 'a') and (ConvertedLetter <= 'z') then
216            begin
217              CharacterCount := CharacterCount + 1;
218              InputString[CharacterCount] := ConvertedLetter
219            end  { if }
220        end;  { while }
221
222      { skip any unread input on the line }
223
224      readln;
225
226      { set the string length }
227
228      StringLength := CharacterCount
229
230    end;  { GetString }
231
{*********************************************************************}
233
234  procedure GenerateKey(InputString : KeyString; StringLength : integer;
235                        var EncipherKey : Key);
236
237    {------------------------------------------------------------------}
238    {  GenerateKey is called to generate the enciphering key from the  }
239    {  input string entered by the user.  It uses an internal procedure }
240    {  PutInKey to insert each letter from the input string into the    }
241    {  key being constructed, unless that character is already present  }
242    {  in the key.  Then it uses PutInKey to insert letters 'z'...'a'   }
243    {  into the key (unless they are already present) to account for    }
244    {  letters not in the input string.                                }
245    {                                                                  }
246    {  Input parameters:                                               }
247    {    InputString - the string of letters entered by the user       }
248    {    StringLength - the length of InputString                      }
249    {                                                                  }
250    {  Output parameters:                                              }
251    {    EncipherKey - the enciphering key generated from InputString  }
252    {------------------------------------------------------------------}
253
254    var
255      Letter : char;              { used as subscript and working variable }
```

```
256        I : integer;              { used as subscript for InputString }
257
258   {++++++++++++++++++++++++++++++++++++++++++++++++++++++++++++++++++++++}
259
260      procedure PutInKey(var EncipherKey : Key; Character : char);
261
262        {---------------------------------------------------------------}
263        {  PutInKey is called with each character that is a candidate to be }
264        {  placed into the enciphering key.  PutInKey scans the letters    }
265        {  that are already in the key.  If the character to be inserted is }
266        {  already present, it is ignored; otherwise, it is inserted at the }
267        {  first unused position in the key.  It is assumed that unused    }
268        {  positions in the key being constructed have been set to blanks.  }
269        {                                                                 }
270        {  Input parameters:                                              }
271        {    EncipherKey - the partially constructed key.  Letters that are }
272        {                  already in EncipherKey are assumed to appear at }
273        {                  the beginning of the key, followed by blanks.   }
274        {    Character - the character that is a candidate to be inserted  }
275        {                into EncipherKey                                 }
276        {                                                                 }
277        {  Output parameters:                                             }
278        {    EncipherKey - the partially constructed key, with Character   }
279        {                  added unless it was already present            }
280        {---------------------------------------------------------------}
281          var
282            Searching : boolean;       { searching for place to insert Character }
283            Letter : char;             { used as subscript for EncipherKey }
284
285        begin  { PutInKey }
286
287            Searching := true;
288            Letter := 'a';
289
290            { scan EncipherKey until Character  or blank is found.  if a blank
291              is found, replace it with Character }
292
293            while Searching do
294              begin
295                if EncipherKey[Letter] = Character then
296
297                    { Character is already present -- stop searching }
298
299                    Searching := false
300
301                else if EncipherKey[Letter] = ' ' then
302                  begin
303
304                    { a blank was found.  replace it with Character and
305                      stop searching }
306
307                    EncipherKey[Letter] := Character;
308                    Searching := false
```

```
309                          end   { if blank was found }
310
311                       else
312
313                          { neither Character or blank found yet -- go on to the
314                             next letter in EncipherKey }
315
316                          Letter := succ(Letter)
317
318                    end   { while }
319
320              end;   { PutInKey }
321
322    {+++++++++++++++++++++++++++++++++++++++++++++++++++++++++++++++++++++}
323
324       begin   { GenerateKey }
325
326          { initialize EncipherKey to all blanks }
327
328          for Letter := 'a' to 'z' do
329            EncipherKey[Letter] := ' ';
330
331          { insert letters from InputString into EncipherKey }
332
333          for I := 1 to StringLength do
334            PutInKey(EncipherKey,InputString[I]);
335
336          { insert letters 'z', 'y',...,'a' not already in EncipherKey }
337
338          for Letter := 'z' downto 'a' do
339            PutInKey(EncipherKey,Letter)
340
341       end;   { GenerateKey }
342
343    {*******************************************************************}
344
345    procedure ConvertKey(EncipherKey : Key; var DecipherKey : Key);
346
347       {------------------------------------------------------------------}
348       {  ConvertKey generates the deciphering key that corresponds to a  }
349       {  given enciphering key.  It operates by scanning the letters in   }
350       {  the enciphering key.  For each letter, it makes the "inverse"    }
351       {  entry in the deciphering key.  For example, if EncipherKey['a']  }
352       {  is equal to 'j', then 'A' is entered in DecipherKey['j'].        }
353       {                                                                   }
354       {  Input parameters:                                                }
355       {     EncipherKey - the enciphering key                             }
356       {                                                                   }
357       {  Output parameters:                                              }
358       {     DecipherKey - the corresponding deciphering key              }
359       {------------------------------------------------------------------}
360
361       var
```

```
362          Letter : char;           { used as subscript for EncipherKey }
363          CipherLetter : char;     { the character at position Letter in EncipherKey }
364
365       begin  { ConvertKey }
366
367          for Letter := 'a' to 'z' do
368            begin
369
370              { CipherLetter is the character at position Letter in EncipherKey }
371
372              CipherLetter := EncipherKey[Letter];
373
374              { enter Letter, converted to upper case, in position CipherLetter
375                of DecipherKey }
376
377              DecipherKey[CipherLetter] := Uppercase(Letter)
378            end
379
380       end;  { ConvertKey }
381
382    {*****************************************************************}
383
384    procedure WriteKeys(EncipherKey : Key; DecipherKey : Key);
385
386       {---------------------------------------------------------------}
387       {  WriteKeys is called at the end of the program.  It writes the }
388       {  generated enciphering and deciphering keys to the file KEYS,  }
389       {  and also displays these keys on the terminal.                 }
390       {                                                               }
391       {  Input parameters:                                             }
392       {    EncipherKey - the generated enciphering key                 }
393       {    DecipherKey - the generated deciphering key                 }
394       {                                                               }
395       {  Output parameters: None                                      }
396       {---------------------------------------------------------------}
397
398       var
399         Letter : char;         { used as subscript for EncipherKey and DecipherKey }
400
401       begin  { WriteKeys }
402
403          { write enciphering key to KEYS and to terminal }
404
405          write('Enciphering key is  ');
406          for Letter := 'a' to 'z' do
407            begin
408              write(EncipherKey[Letter]);
409              write(KEYS,EncipherKey[Letter])
410            end;
411          writeln;
412          writeln(KEYS);
413
414          { write deciphering key to KEYS and to terminal }
```

```
415
416        write('Deciphering key is  ');
417        for Letter := 'a' to 'z' do
418          begin
419            write(DecipherKey[Letter]);
420            write(KEYS,DecipherKey[Letter])
421          end;
422        writeln;
423        writeln(KEYS)
424
425      end;  { WriteKeys }
426
427   {**********************************************************************}
428
429   procedure CleanUp;
430
431      {------------------------------------------------------------------}
432      {  CleanUp is called once at the end of the program.  It closes    }
433      {  the file KEYS, if this is required in the Pascal version being   }
434      {  used, and waits for the user to enter a carriage return before  }
435      {  exiting the program.                                            }
436      {------------------------------------------------------------------}
437
438      begin  { CleanUp }
439
440         { ## Non-standard statements -- Turbo Pascal version }
441
442         close(KEYS);
443
444         { End Turbo Pascal version }
445
446         write('Press return to exit program');
447         readln
448
449      end;  { CleanUp}
450
451   {**********************************************************************}
452
453   begin  { main program }
454
455      Initialize;
456
457      { get input string from terminal }
458
459      GetString(InputString,StringLength);
460
461      { generate enciphering and deciphering keys }
462
463      GenerateKey(InputString,StringLength,EncipherKey);
464      ConvertKey(EncipherKey,DecipherKey);
465
466      { write keys to file and to terminal }
467
```

```
468      WriteKeys(EncipherKey,DecipherKey);
469      CleanUp
470
471    end.
```

EXAMPLE PROGRAM

Letters1

```
1    program Letters1(input,output,TEXTDATA);
2
3    {------------------------------------------------------------------}
4    {  This program reads an input file and counts the number of       }
5    {  times each letter of the alphabet occurs in this file.  It writes }
6    {  an alphabetical listing that shows the total number of occurrences }
7    {  of each letter, the relative frequency of each letter, and the  }
8    {  total number of occurrences of all letters.                     }
9    {                                                                  }
10   {  Capitalization of letters is not considered significant -- for  }
11   {  example, 'A' and 'a' are considered to be the same letter for the }
12   {  purposes of letter count and frequency calculations.  Characters }
13   {  in the input file that are not alphabetic are ignored.          }
14   {                                                                  }
15   {  Terminal screen control routines are used to clear the screen   }
16   {  initially, and to position the cursor so that the output listing }
17   {  appears in two columns.                                         }
18   {                                                                  }
19   {  Input :   File TEXTDATA, containing the characters which are to  }
20   {            be counted.                                           }
21   {                                                                  }
22   {  Output :  An alphabetical listing showing the total number of   }
23   {            occurrences, and the relative frequency of occurrence, }
24   {            of each letter of the alphabet in the input file.     }
25   {                                                                  }
26   {  This program contains non-standard Pascal statements to support }
27   {  Turbo Pascal and Berkeley Pascal versions.  Non-standard Pascal }
28   {  statements appear in the following locations:                   }
29   {     1. in the 'uses' clause immediately following this comment block }
30   {     2. in the screen control procedures ClearScreen and MoveCursor }
31   {     3. in procedures Initialize and CleanUp                      }
32   {  These non-standard statements are preceded by a comment that    }
33   {  begins with '## N'.                                             }
34   {------------------------------------------------------------------}
35
36      { ## Non-standard statements -- Turbo Pascal version }
37
38      uses Crt;
39
40      { End Turbo Pascal version }
41
42
43   type
```

```
44       CountOfLetters = array ['a'..'z'] of integer;
45
46    var
47       TEXTDATA : text;                  { input file }
48       LetterCounts : CountOfLetters;    { count of occurrences of each letter }
49       Character : char;                 { used as subscript for LetterCounts }
50       TotalLetters : integer;           { total number of letters counted }
51
52    {*********************************************************************}
53
54    function Lowercase(Letter : char) : char;
55
56       {-----------------------------------------------------------------}
57       {   Lowercase is used to convert alphabetic characters to lower    }
58       {   case.  If the input parameter is an upper case letter          }
59       {   ('A' through 'Z'), the value of the function is the corresponding}
60       {   lower case letter ('a' through 'z').  If the input parameter is }
61       {   any other character, the value of the function is equal to the  }
62       {   input parameter.                                               }
63       {                                                                  }
64       {   Input parameters:                                              }
65       {     Letter - character to be converted to lower case             }
66       {                                                                  }
67       {   Output parameters : None                                       }
68       {                                                                  }
69       {   Function value : the value of the input parameter Letter,      }
70       {                    converted to lower case if it was originally  }
71       {                    in the range 'A' through 'Z'                  }
72       {-----------------------------------------------------------------}
73
74       var
75          ConvertedLetter : char;      { the function value being computed }
76          DistancePastA : integer;     { the distance in the alphabet between
77                                         the letter being converted and 'A' }
78       begin  { Lowercase }
79
80          { if the input parameter is an upper case letter, convert it to
81            the corresponding lower case letter.  otherwise, the converted
82            letter is set equal to the input parameter. }
83
84          if (Letter >= 'A') and (Letter <= 'Z') then
85             begin
86                DistancePastA := ord(Letter) - ord('A');
87                ConvertedLetter := chr(ord('a') + DistancePastA)
88             end  { if }
89          else
90             ConvertedLetter := Letter;
91
92          { set the function value }
93
94          Lowercase := ConvertedLetter
95
96       end;  { Lowercase }
```

```
97
98      {***********************************************************}
99
100     { ## Non-standard statements -- Berkeley Pascal version }
101     {
102     procedure ClrScr; external;
103     }
104     { End Berkeley Pascal version }
105
106     procedure ClearScreen;
107
108        {-----------------------------------------------------------}
109        {  ClearScreen clears the terminal screen and positions the }
110        {  cursor at the upper left corner of the screen.  It calls a }
111        {  non-standard Pascal library routine to perform this operation. }
112        {-----------------------------------------------------------}
113
114        begin
115
116           ClrScr    { call library routine ClrScr to clear screen }
117
118        end;  { ClearScreen }
119
120     {***********************************************************}
121
122     { ## Non-standard statements -- Berkeley Pascal version }
123     {
124     procedure GotoXY(X, Y : integer); external;
125     }
126     { End Berkeley Pascal version }
127
128     procedure MoveCursor(Row, Col : integer);
129
130        {-----------------------------------------------------------}
131        {  MoveCursor moves the cursor on the terminal screen to the }
132        {  row and column given by its input parameters.  The next write }
133        {  or writeln operation that sends output to the terminal will }
134        {  begin writing at the row and column location designated.  The }
135        {  procedure calls a non-standard Pascal library routine to perform }
136        {  this operation. }
137        {
138        {  Input parameters: }
139        {    Row,Col - the row (line) and column (horizontal position) on }
140        {              the screen to which the cursor is to be moved.  The }
141        {              upper left-hand corner of the screen is row 1, column 1. }
142        {-----------------------------------------------------------}
143
144        begin
145
146           { call library routine GotoXY to move the cursor -- note that }
147             GotoXY expects the column value as its first parameter }
148
149        GotoXY(Col,Row)
```

```
150
151       end;   { MoveCursor }
152
153    {*********************************************************************}
154
155    procedure Initialize(var LetterCounts : CountOfLetters;
156                          var TotalLetters : integer);
157
158       {---------------------------------------------------------------}
159       {  Initialize is called once at the beginning of the program.  It  }
160       {  opens the input file TEXTDATA and initializes the total number  }
161       {  of letters and the array of letter counts to zero.              }
162       {                                                                  }
163       {  Input parameters : None                                         }
164       {                                                                  }
165       {  Output parameters:                                              }
166       {     LetterCounts - initialized to all zeros                      }
167       {     TotalLetters - initialized to zero                           }
168       {---------------------------------------------------------------}
169
170       var
171         Character : char;             { used as subscript for LetterCounts }
172
173       begin  { initialize }
174
175         { ## Non-standard statements -- Turbo Pascal version }
176
177           assign(TEXTDATA,'TEXTDATA');
178
179         { End Turbo Pascal version }
180
181         { open data file }
182
183         reset(TEXTDATA);
184
185         { initialize total letters and all letter counts to all zero }
186
187         TotalLetters := 0;
188         for Character := 'a' to 'z' do
189           LetterCounts[Character] := 0
190
191       end;  { Initialize }
192
193    {*********************************************************************}
194
195    procedure CountCharacters(var LetterCounts : CountOfLetters;
196                          var TotalLetters : integer);
197
198       {---------------------------------------------------------------}
199       {  CountCharacters is called once.  It reads TEXTDATA, one character}
200       {  at a time, until end-of-file.  For each alphabetic character     }
201       {  read, it adds one to the corresponding count in LetterCounts.    }
202       {  After all letters have been counted, the total number of letters }
```

```
203        {  is calculated and stored in TotalLetters.                      }
204        {                                                                  }
205        {  Input parameters:                                              }
206        {     LetterCounts - all counts assumed to be initialized to zero }
207        {     TotalLetters - assumed to be initialized to zero            }
208        {                                                                  }
209        {  Output parameters:                                            }
210        {     LetterCounts - counts of each alphabetic character in TEXTDATA }
211        {     TotalLetters - the total number of letters counted          }
212        {------------------------------------------------------------------}
213
214     var
215        Character : char;       { character read from TEXTDATA }
216        Letter : char;          { used as subscript for LetterCounts }
217
218     begin   { CountCharacters }
219
220        { read TEXTDATA, one character at a time, until end-of-file }
221
222        while not eof(TEXTDATA) do
223          begin
224            if eoln(TEXTDATA) then
225
226              { if the end of a line has been reached, go to the next line }
227
228              readln(TEXTDATA)
229            else
230              begin
231
232                { if end of line has not been reached, read the next
233                  character and convert it to lower case }
234
235                read(TEXTDATA,Character);
236                Character := Lowercase(Character);
237
238                { if the converted character is 'a' through 'z', add one
239                  to the corresponding count in LetterCounts }
240
241                if (Character >= 'a') and (Character <= 'z') then
242                  LetterCounts[Character] := LetterCounts[Character] + 1
243              end   { else }
244          end;   { while }
245
246        { calculate the total number of letters counted }
247
248        for Letter := 'a' to 'z' do
249          TotalLetters := TotalLetters + LetterCounts[Letter]
250
251     end;   { CountCharacters }
252
253   {*******************************************************************}
254
255   procedure WriteResults(LetterCounts : CountOfLetters; TotalLetters : integer);
```

```
256
257        {----------------------------------------------------------------------}
258        {  WriteResults is called once at the end of the program.  It        }
259        {  displays a table of letters, in alphabetical order, with the      }
260        {  number of occurrences and relative frequency of each letter.      }
261        {  Screen control routines are called to clear the screen and to     }
262        {  position the cursor to display the table in two columns.          }
263        {                                                                    }
264        {  Input parameters:                                                 }
265        {    LetterCounts - count of number of occurrences of each letter    }
266        {    TotalLetters - total number of letters counted                 }
267        {                                                                    }
268        {  Output parameters: None                                          }
269        {----------------------------------------------------------------------}
270
271        var
272           Character : char;          { used as subscript for LetterCounts }
273           LineNumber : integer;      { count of number of lines written }
274           Frequency : real;          { relative frequency of current letter }
275
276        begin  { WriteResults }
277
278           { clear terminal screen and write headings }
279
280           ClearScreen;
281           writeln('Letter   Count    Frequency        Letter   Count    Frequency');
282
283           { first line to be written is line number 1 }
284
285           LineNumber := 1;
286
287           { display letter counts and frequencies }
288
289           for Character := 'a' to 'z' do
290             begin
291
292                { position cursor in the left-hand column for lines 1-13, or in
293                  the right-hand column for lines 14-26 }
294
295                if LineNumber <= 13 then
296                  MoveCursor(LineNumber+2,4)
297                else
298                  MoveCursor(LineNumber-11,40);
299
300                { write letter, count, and relative frequency }
301
302                write(Character,LetterCounts[Character]:10);
303                Frequency := LetterCounts[Character] / TotalLetters;
304                writeln(Frequency:12:2);
305
306                { update line number }
307
308                LineNumber := LineNumber + 1
```

```
309      end;  { for }
310
311        { move cursor to bottom of table and write total letter count }
312
313        MoveCursor(17,1);
314        writeln('Total letters = ',TotalLetters)
315
316     end;  { WriteResults }
317
318  {********************************************************************}
319
320  procedure CleanUp;
321
322     {------------------------------------------------------------------}
323     {  CleanUp is called once, at the end of the program.  It closes   }
324     {  the input file, if this is required in the Pascal version being  }
325     {  used, and waits for the user to enter a carriage return before   }
326     {  exiting the program.                                            }
327     {------------------------------------------------------------------}
328
329     begin
330
331        { ## Non-standard statements -- Turbo Pascal version }
332
333        close(TEXTDATA);
334
335        { End Turbo Pascal version }
336
337        write('Press return to exit program');
338        readln
339
340     end;
341
342  {********************************************************************}
343
344  begin   { main program }
345
346     Initialize(LetterCounts,TotalLetters);
347
348     { read input file and count alphabetic characters }
349
350     CountCharacters(LetterCounts,TotalLetters);
351
352     { display table of results }
353
354     WriteResults(LetterCounts,TotalLetters);
355     CleanUp
356
357  end.
```

EXAMPLE PROGRAM
Letters2

```
 1   program Letters2(input,output,TEXTDATA);
 2
 3   {---------------------------------------------------------------------}
 4   {  This program reads an input file and counts the number of          }
 5   {  times each letter of the alphabet occurs in this file.  It writes  }
 6   {  a listing that shows the total number of occurrences of each       }
 7   {  letter, the relative frequency of each letter, and the total       }
 8   {  number of occurrences of all letters.  The listing is ordered by   }
 9   {  the relative frequency of the letters.                             }
10   {                                                                     }
11   {  Capitalization of letters is not considered significant -- for     }
12   {  example, 'A' and 'a' are considered to be the same letter for the  }
13   {  purposes of letter count and frequency calculations.  Characters   }
14   {  in the input file that are not alphabetic are ignored.             }
15   {                                                                     }
16   {  Terminal screen control routines are used to clear the screen      }
17   {  initially, and to position the cursor so that the output listing   }
18   {  appears in two columns.                                            }
19   {                                                                     }
20   {  Input :    File TEXTDATA, containing the characters which are to   }
21   {             be counted.                                             }
22   {                                                                     }
23   {  Output :   A listing showing the total number of occurrences and   }
24   {             the relative frequency of occurrence of each letter of  }
25   {             the alphabet in the input file, ordered by frequency.   }
26   {                                                                     }
27   {  This program contains non-standard Pascal statements to support    }
28   {  Turbo Pascal and Berkeley Pascal versions.  Non-standard Pascal    }
29   {  statements appear in the following locations:                      }
30   {     1. in the 'uses' clause immediately following this comment block }
31   {     2. in the screen control procedures ClearScreen and MoveCursor  }
32   {     3. in procedures Initialize and CleanUp                         }
33   {  These non-standard statements are preceded by a comment that       }
34   {  begins with '## N'.                                                }
35   {                                                                     }
36   {  Modification history:                                              }
37   {      This program performs the same letter counting operations as   }
38   {      the original version (program Letters1).  However, it displays }
39   {      a table of results that is sorted by letter frequency.  A      }
40   {      simple exchange sort is used to order the table for display.   }
41   {---------------------------------------------------------------------}
42
43      { ## Non-standard statements -- Turbo Pascal version }
```

```
44
45        uses Crt;
46
47        { End Turbo Pascal version }
48
49     type
50        CountOfLetters = array ['a'..'z'] of integer;
51
52        LetterStats = record                { entry in table used for sorting }
53                        Letter : char;         { letter of the alphabet }
54                        Count : integer        { count of occurrences of that letter }
55                      end;
56
57        ListOfCounts = array [1..26] of LetterStats;
58
59     var
60        TEXTDATA : text;                   { input file }
61        LetterCounts : CountOfLetters;     { count of occurrences of each letter }
62        Character : char;                  { used as subscript for LetterCounts }
63        TotalLetters : integer;            { total number of letters counted }
64        LetterList : ListOfCounts;         { table used for sorting by frequency }
65
66     {*******************************************************************}
67
68     function Lowercase(Letter : char) : char;
69
70        {-----------------------------------------------------------------}
71        {   Lowercase is used to convert alphabetic characters to lower    }
72        {   case.  If the input parameter is an upper case letter          }
73        {   ('A' through 'Z'), the value of the function is the corresponding}
74        {   lower case letter ('a' through 'z').  If the input parameter is }
75        {   any other character, the value of the function is equal to the  }
76        {   input parameter.                                                }
77        {                                                                   }
78        {   Input parameters:                                               }
79        {     Letter - character to be converted to lower case             }
80        {                                                                   }
81        {   Output parameters : None                                        }
82        {                                                                   }
83        {   Function value : the value of the input parameter Letter,       }
84        {                    converted to lower case if it was originally   }
85        {                    in the range 'A' through 'Z'                   }
86        {-----------------------------------------------------------------}
87
88        var
89           ConvertedLetter : char;        { the function value being computed }
90           DistancePastA : integer;       { the distance in the alphabet between
91                                            the letter being converted and 'A' }
92        begin  { Lowercase }
93
94           { if the input parameter is an upper case letter, convert it to
95             the corresponding lower case letter.  otherwise, the converted
96             letter is set equal to the input parameter. }
```

```
 97
 98          if (Letter >= 'A') and (Letter <= 'Z') then
 99            begin
100              DistancePastA := ord(Letter) - ord('A');
101              ConvertedLetter := chr(ord('a') + DistancePastA)
102            end  { if }
103          else
104            ConvertedLetter := Letter;
105
106          { set the function value }
107
108          Lowercase := ConvertedLetter
109
110       end;  { Lowercase }
111
112  {*********************************************************************}
113
114  { ## Non-standard statements -- Berkeley Pascal version }
115  {
116  procedure ClrScr; external;
117  }
118  { End Berkeley Pascal version }
119
120  procedure ClearScreen;
121
122     {-------------------------------------------------------------------}
123     {  ClearScreen clears the terminal screen and positions the         }
124     {  cursor at the upper left corner of the screen.  It calls a        }
125     {  non-standard Pascal library routine to perform this operation.    }
126     {-------------------------------------------------------------------}
127
128     begin
129
130       ClrScr   { call library routine ClrScr to clear screen }
131
132     end;  { ClearScreen }
133
134  {*********************************************************************}
135
136  { ## Non-standard statements -- Berkeley Pascal version }
137  {
138  procedure GotoXY(X, Y : integer); external;
139  }
140  { End Berkeley Pascal version }
141
142  procedure MoveCursor(Row, Col : integer);
143
144     {-------------------------------------------------------------------}
145     {  MoveCursor moves the cursor on the terminal screen to the        }
146     {  row and column given by its input parameters.  The next write    }
147     {  or writeln operation that sends output to the terminal will      }
148     {  begin writing at the row and column location designated.  The    }
149     {  procedure calls a non-standard Pascal library routine to perform }
```

```
150      {  this operation.                                              }
151      {                                                              }
152      {  Input parameters:                                           }
153      {    Row,Col - the row (line) and column (horizontal position) on  }
154      {            the screen to which the cursor is to be moved.  The  }
155      {            upper left-hand corner of the screen is row 1, column 1. }
156      {--------------------------------------------------------------}
157
158      begin
159
160         { call library routine GotoXY to move the cursor -- note that
161           GotoXY expects the column value as its first parameter }
162
163         GotoXY(Col,Row)
164
165      end;   { MoveCursor }
166
167   {**********************************************************************}
168
169   procedure Initialize(var LetterCounts : CountOfLetters;
170                        var TotalLetters : integer);
171
172      {--------------------------------------------------------------}
173      {  Initialize is called once at the beginning of the program.  It  }
174      {  opens the input file TEXTDATA and initializes the total number  }
175      {  of letters and the array of letter counts to zero.          }
176      {                                                              }
177      {  Input parameters : None                                     }
178      {                                                              }
179      {  Output parameters:                                          }
180      {    LetterCounts - initialized to all zeros                   }
181      {    TotalLetters - initialized to zero                        }
182      {--------------------------------------------------------------}
183
184      var
185        Character : char;              { used as subscript for LetterCounts }
186
187      begin  { initialize }
188
189         { ## Non-standard statements -- Turbo Pascal version }
190
191            assign(TEXTDATA,'TEXTDATA');
192
193         { End Turbo Pascal version }
194
195         { open data file }
196
197         reset(TEXTDATA);
198
199         { initialize total letters and all letter counts to all zero }
200
201         TotalLetters := 0;
202         for Character := 'a' to 'z' do
```

```
203              LetterCounts[Character] := 0
204
205        end;  { Initialize }
206
207    {***********************************************************************}
208
209    procedure CountCharacters(var LetterCounts : CountOfLetters;
210                                  var TotalLetters : integer);
211
212        {----------------------------------------------------------------}
213        {  CountCharacters is called once.  It reads TEXTDATA, one character}
214        {  at a time, until end-of-file.  For each alphabetic character   }
215        {  read, it adds one to the corresponding count in LetterCounts.  }
216        {  After all letters have been counted, the total number of letters }
217        {  is calculated and stored in TotalLetters.                     }
218        {                                                                }
219        {  Input parameters:                                             }
220        {    LetterCounts - all counts assumed to be initialized to zero }
221        {    TotalLetters - assumed to be initialized to zero            }
222        {                                                                }
223        {  Output parameters:                                            }
224        {    LetterCounts - counts of each alphabetic character in TEXTDATA }
225        {    TotalLetters - the total number of letters counted          }
226        {----------------------------------------------------------------}
227
228    var
229        Character : char;      { character read from TEXTDATA }
230        Letter : char;         { used as subscript for LetterCounts }
231
232    begin  { CountCharacters }
233
234        { read TEXTDATA, one character at a time, until end-of-file }
235
236        while not eof(TEXTDATA) do
237          begin
238            if eoln(TEXTDATA) then
239
240              { if the end of a line has been reached, go to the next line }
241
242              readln(TEXTDATA)
243            else
244              begin
245
246                { if end of line has not been reached, read the next
247                  character and convert it to lower case }
248
249                read(TEXTDATA,Character);
250                Character := Lowercase(Character);
251
252                { if the converted character is 'a' through 'z', add one
253                  to the corresponding count in LetterCounts }
254
255                if (Character >= 'a') and (Character <= 'z') then
```

```
256                    LetterCounts[Character] := LetterCounts[Character] + 1
257               end  { else }
258           end;  { while }
259
260        { calculate the total number of letters counted }
261
262        for Letter := 'a' to 'z' do
263          TotalLetters := TotalLetters + LetterCounts[Letter]
264
265      end;  { CountCharacters }
266
267  {*********************************************************************}
268
269  procedure BuildSortedList (LetterCounts : CountOfLetters;
270                             var LetterList : ListOfCounts);
271
272     {-----------------------------------------------------------------}
273     {  BuildSortedList inserts each letter and the number of occurrences}
274     {  of that letter into the array LetterList.  The entries in       }
275     {  LetterList are then sorted by number of occurrences, using a    }
276     {  simple exchange sort.                                           }
277     {                                                                 }
278     {  Input parameters:                                              }
279     {    LetterCounts - number of occurrences of each letter          }
280     {                                                                 }
281     {  Output parameters:                                             }
282     {    LetterList - list of letters and number of occurrences, sorted }
283     {                 by number of occurrences                        }
284     {-----------------------------------------------------------------}
285
286     var
287        Character : char;         { used as subscript for LetterCounts }
288        I : integer;              { used as subscript for LetterList }
289        Start : integer;          { Start and Compare are subscripts that   }
290        Compare : integer;        {   indicate entries in LetterList being  }
291                                  {   compared during the exchange sort     }
292        Hold : LetterStats;       { temporary variable used while exchanging two }
293                                  {   entries in LetterList                 }
294
295     begin  { BuildSortedList }
296
297        { enter each letter and its number of occurrences into LetterList.
298          Character is used as a subscript for LetterCounts, I as a subscript
299          for LetterList }
300
301        Character := 'a';
302        for I := 1 to 26 do
303          begin
304            LetterList[I].Letter := Character;
305            LetterList[I].Count := LetterCounts[Character];
306            Character := succ(Character)
307          end;
308
```

```
309            { sort the entries in LetterList by number of occurrences }
310
311         for Start := 1 to 25 do
312           for Compare := Start+1 to 26 do
313
314              { Start and Compare are subscripts indicating entries in
315                 LetterList, with Start preceding Compare in the array. }
316
317              if LetterList[Start].Count < LetterList[Compare].Count then
318                begin
319
320                   { if the number of occurrences in entry Start is less then
321                      the number of occurrences in entry Compare, exchange these
322                      two entries. }
323
324                   Hold := LetterList[Start];
325                   LetterList[Start] := LetterList[Compare];
326                   LetterList[Compare] := Hold
327                end
328
329      end;  { BuildSortedList }
330
331    {*********************************************************************}
332
333    procedure WriteResults(LetterList : ListOfCounts; TotalLetters : integer);
334
335       {-------------------------------------------------------------------}
336       {  WriteResults is called once at the end of the program.  It       }
337       {  displays a table of letters, with the number of occurrences and  }
338       {  relative frequency of each letter, sorted by frequency.          }
339       {  Screen control routines are called to clear the screen and to    }
340       {  position the cursor to display the table in two columns.         }
341       {                                                                   }
342       {  Input parameters:                                                }
343       {    LetterList - table containing number of occurrences of each    }
344       {                  letter, sorted by number of occurrences          }
345       {    TotalLetters - total number of letters counted                 }
346       {                                                                   }
347       {  Output parameters: None                                          }
348       {-------------------------------------------------------------------}
349
350       var
351         LineNumber : integer;      { count of number of lines written }
352         Frequency : real;          { relative frequency of current letter }
353
354       begin  { WriteResults }
355
356          { clear terminal screen and write headings }
357
358          ClearScreen;
359          writeln('Letter   Count    Frequency        Letter   Count    Frequency');
360
361          { display letter counts and frequencies }
```

```
362
363        for LineNumber := 1 to 26 do
364          begin
365
366             { position cursor in the left-hand column for lines 1-13, or in
367               the right-hand column for lines 14-26 }
368
369             if LineNumber <= 13 then
370               MoveCursor(LineNumber+2,4)
371             else
372               MoveCursor(LineNumber-11,40);
373
374             { write letter, count, and relative frequency }
375
376             write(LetterList[LineNumber].Letter,LetterList[LineNumber].Count:10);
377             Frequency := LetterList[LineNumber].Count / TotalLetters;
378             writeln(Frequency:12:2)
379           end;  { for }
380
381        { move cursor to bottom of table and write total letter count }
382
383        MoveCursor(17,1);
384        writeln('Total letters = ',TotalLetters)
385
386      end;  { WriteResults }
387
388  {*******************************************************************}
389
390  procedure CleanUp;
391
392      {----------------------------------------------------------------}
393      { CleanUp is called once, at the end of the program.  It closes   }
394      { the input file, if this is required in the Pascal version being }
395      { used, and waits for the user to enter a carriage return before  }
396      { exiting the program.                                            }
397      {----------------------------------------------------------------}
398
399      begin  { CleanUp }
400        { ## Non-standard statements -- Turbo Pascal version }
401
402        close(TEXTDATA);
403
404        { End Turbo Pascal version }
405
406        write('Press return to exit program');
407        readln
408
409      end;  { CleanUp }
410
411  {*******************************************************************}
412
413    begin  { main program }
414
```

```
415        Initialize(LetterCounts,TotalLetters);
416
417        { read input file and count alphabetic characters }
418
419        CountCharacters(LetterCounts,TotalLetters);
420
421        { build list sorted by number of occurrences }
422
423        BuildSortedList(LetterCounts,LetterList);
424
425        { display table of results }
426
427        WriteResults(LetterList,TotalLetters);
428        CleanUp
429
430     end.
```

EXAMPLE PROGRAM
Solve

```
 1    program Solve(input,output,CRYPTO,CCOUNT);
 2
 3    {-------------------------------------------------------------------------}
 4    {  This program is an interactive tool for solving cryptograms that    }
 5    {  are encoded using a simple substitution cipher.  The program        }
 6    {  displays an encrypted message on the terminal screen, along         }
 7    {  with an indication of which letters occur most frequently in the    }
 8    {  ciphertext.  For ease of reference, the most common letters in      }
 9    {  typical English text are also displayed.  The program then prompts  }
10    {  the user to enter commands in an effort to decode the message.      }
11    {                                                                      }
12    {  The possible commands are                                           }
13    {      S x=y   -  substitute a plaintext letter y for the ciphertext   }
14    {                 letter x wherever it occurs                          }
15    {      H x     -  requests help on ciphertext letter x; the correct    }
16    {                 plaintext letter is substituted for x wherever       }
17    {                 it occurs                                            }
18    {      B x     -  replace the ciphertext letter x by a blank wherever  }
19    {                 it occurs (to erase the effect of a previous         }
20    {                 incorrect S command)                                 }
21    {      Q       -  quit, displaying the correctly deciphered message    }
22    {                                                                      }
23    {  The program shows the effect of each command by displaying a trial }
24    {  plaintext decipherment above the original ciphertext.  The         }
25    {  ciphertext message is displayed using lower case characters, and    }
26    {  the plaintext decipherment is displayed using upper case letters.   }
27    {  Commands may be entered using any combination of upper case and     }
28    {  lower case characters.                                              }
29    {                                                                      }
30    {  Cryptograms for solution are read from the file CRYPTO.  The first }
31    {  line of each cryptogram in CRYPTO gives the deciphering key needed }
32    {  to decode the message.  (Deciphering keys have the same format     }
33    {  used in program Cipher.)  Following the deciphering key are one    }
34    {  or more lines containing the enciphered message.  The end of the   }
35    {  enciphered message is marked by a line containing only the         }
36    {  character '#'.  The enciphered message may not contain the         }
37    {  characters '#' or '&'.                                             }
38    {                                                                      }
39    {  The file CCOUNT controls the sequence in which cryptograms from     }
40    {  CRYPTO are used by the program.  CCOUNT consists of one line that  }
41    {  contains two integers.  The first integer gives the number of the  }
42    {  last cryptogram from CRYPTO that was used, and the second gives    }
43    {  the total number of cryptograms stored in CRYPTO.  When the        }
```

```
44    {  program is executed, it reads these numbers and selects from       }
45    {  CRYPTO the next cryptogram after the one previously used.  If all   }
46    {  cryptograms have been used, the program returns to the first one    }
47    {  in CRYPTO.  CCOUNT is rewritten to reflect the use of the           }
48    {  cryptogram that is selected.                                        }
49    {                                                                      }
50    {  Input:  A cryptogram is read from file CRYPTO, as determined by     }
51    {          the information in CCOUNT.  Commands are read from the      }
52    {          terminal.                                                   }
53    {                                                                      }
54    {  Output: Updated information is rewritten to file CCOUNT.  The       }
55    {          result of executing each command is displayed on the        }
56    {          terminal.                                                   }
57    {                                                                      }
58    {  This program contains non-standard Pascal statements to support     }
59    {  Turbo Pascal and Berkeley Pascal versions.  Non-standard Pascal     }
60    {  statements appear in the following locations:                       }
61    {    1. in the 'uses' clause immediately following this comment block }
62    {    2. in the screen control procedures ClearScreen, ClearLine,       }
63    {       and MoveCursor                                                 }
64    {    3. in procedures Initialize and CleanUp                           }
65    {  These non-standard statements are preceded by a comment that        }
66    {  begins with '## N'.                                                 }
67    {----------------------------------------------------------------------}
68
69    { ## Non-standard statements -- Turbo Pascal version }
70
71    uses Crt;
72
73    { End Turbo Pascal version }
74
75    const
76      MaximumLength = 400;           { maximum length for an enciphered message }
77
78    type
79      Message = array[1..MaximumLength] of char;
80      Key = array['a'..'z'] of char;
81
82      LetterFrequencies = record              { table of letter frequencies }
83                            Letter : char;    { letter of the alphabet }
84                            Frequency : real  { frequency in ciphertext }
85                          end;
86
87      CryptoPuzzle = record                   { cryptogram information }
88            CipherKey : Key;                  { deciphering key }
89            Ciphertext : Message;             { enciphered message }
90            CipherLength : integer;           { length of Ciphertext }
91            CommonLetters : array[1..8]
92                      of LetterFrequencies;   { most common ciphertext letters }
93            Plaintext : Message;              { solution being constructed }
94            Solved : boolean                  { solution is complete }
95          end;  { CryptoPuzzle }
96
```

```
97      CommandInfo = record                    { command information }
98                       CommandCode : char;    { command code }
99                       Parameter1 : char;     { first parameter }
100                      Parameter2 : char      { second parameter }
101                  end;  { CommandInfo }
102
103     var
104       CRYPTO : text;                        { file containing cryptograms }
105       CCOUNT : text;                        { record of cryptograms used }
106       Cryptogram : CryptoPuzzle;            { current cryptogram }
107       Command : CommandInfo;                { current command }
108
109     {********************************************************************}
110
111     { ## Non-standard statements -- Berkeley Pascal version }
112     {
113     procedure ClrScr; external;
114     }
115     { End Berkeley Pascal version }
116
117     procedure ClearScreen;
118
119        {-------------------------------------------------------------}
120        {  ClearScreen clears the terminal screen and positions the   }
121        {  cursor at the upper left corner of the screen.  It calls a  }
122        {  non-standard Pascal library routine to perform this operation. }
123        {-------------------------------------------------------------}
124
125        begin
126
127          ClrScr    { call library routine ClrScr to clear screen }
128
129        end;  { ClearScreen }
130
131     {********************************************************************}
132
133     { ## Non-standard statements -- Berkeley Pascal version }
134     {
135     procedure GotoXY(X, Y : integer); external;
136     }
137     { End Berkeley Pascal version }
138
139     procedure MoveCursor(Row, Col : integer);
140
141        {-------------------------------------------------------------}
142        {  MoveCursor moves the cursor on the terminal screen to the   }
143        {  row and column given by its input parameters.  The next write }
144        {  or writeln operation that sends output to the terminal will }
145        {  begin writing at the row and column location designated.  The }
146        {  procedure calls a non-standard Pascal library routine to perform }
147        {  this operation.                                             }
148        {                                                             }
149        {  Input parameters:                                          }
```

```
150       {     Row,Col - the row (line) and column (horizontal position) on    }
151       {           the screen to which the cursor is to be moved.  The       }
152       {           upper left-hand corner of the screen is row 1, column 1. }
153       {----------------------------------------------------------------}
154
155       begin
156
157          { call library routine GotoXY to move the cursor -- note that
158            GotoXY expects the column value as its first parameter }
159
160          GotoXY(Col,Row)
161
162       end;   { MoveCursor }
163
164    {********************************************************************}
165
166    { ## Non-standard statements -- Berkeley Pascal version }
167    {
168    procedure ClrEol; external;
169    }
170    { End Berkeley Pascal version }
171
172    procedure ClearLine;
173
174       {----------------------------------------------------------------}
175       {  ClearLine clears the line on the terminal screen where the     }
176       {  cursor is currently positioned, from the cursor position to the }
177       {  end of the line.  It calls a non-standard Pascal library routine }
178       {  to perform this function.                                       }
179       {----------------------------------------------------------------}
180
181       begin
182
183          ClrEol      { call library routine ClrEol to clear line }
184
185       end;   { ClearLine }
186
187    {********************************************************************}
188
189    function Lowercase(Letter : char) : char;
190
191       {----------------------------------------------------------------}
192       {  Lowercase is used to convert alphabetic characters to lower     }
193       {  case.  If the input parameter is an upper case letter           }
194       {  ('A' through 'Z'), the value of the function is the corresponding}
195       {  lower case letter ('a' through 'z').  If the input parameter is  }
196       {  any other character, the value of the function is equal to the   }
197       {  input parameter.                                                 }
198       {                                                                   }
199       {  Input parameters:                                                }
200       {     Letter - character to be converted to lower case              }
201       {                                                                   }
202       {  Output parameters : None                                         }
```

```
203    {                                                                  }
204    {  Function value : the value of the input parameter Letter,       }
205    {                   converted to lower case if it was originally   }
206    {                   in the range 'A' through 'Z'                    }
207    {------------------------------------------------------------------}
208
209    var
210      ConvertedLetter : char;        { the function value being computed }
211      DistancePastA : integer;       { the distance in the alphabet between
212                                       the letter being converted and 'A' }
213    begin  { Lowercase }
214
215      { if the input parameter is an upper case letter, convert it to
216        the corresponding lower case letter.  otherwise, the converted
217        letter is set equal to the input parameter. }
218
219      if Letter in ['A'..'Z'] then
220        begin
221          DistancePastA := ord(Letter) - ord('A');
222          ConvertedLetter := chr(ord('a') + DistancePastA)
223        end  { if }
224      else
225        ConvertedLetter := Letter;
226
227      { set the function value }
228
229      Lowercase := ConvertedLetter
230
231    end;  { Lowercase }
232
233  {*******************************************************************}
234
235  function Uppercase(Letter : char) : char;
236
237    {------------------------------------------------------------------}
238    {  Uppercase is used to convert alphabetic characters to upper     }
239    {  case.  If the input parameter is a lower case letter            }
240    {  ('a' through 'z'), the value of the function is the corresponding}
241    {  upper case letter ('A' through 'Z').  If the input parameter is }
242    {  any other character, the value of the function is equal to the  }
243    {  input parameter.                                                }
244    {                                                                  }
245    {  Input parameters:                                               }
246    {    Letter - character to be converted to upper case              }
247    {                                                                  }
248    {  Output parameters : None                                        }
249    {                                                                  }
250    {  Function value : the value of the input parameter Letter,       }
251    {                   converted to upper case if it was originally   }
252    {                   in the range 'a' through 'z'                    }
253    {------------------------------------------------------------------}
254
255    var
```

```
256        ConvertedLetter : char;          { the function value being computed }
257        DistancePastA : integer;         { the distance in the alphabet between
258                                            the letter being converted and 'a' }
259     begin  { Uppercase }
260
261        { if the input parameter is a lower case letter, convert it to
262          the corresponding upper case letter.  otherwise, the converted
263          letter is set equal to the input parameter. }
264
265        if Letter in ['a'..'z'] then
266          begin
267            DistancePastA := ord(Letter) - ord('a');
268            ConvertedLetter := chr(ord('A') + DistancePastA)
269          end  { if }
270        else
271          ConvertedLetter := Letter;
272
273        { set the function value }
274
275        Uppercase := ConvertedLetter
276
277     end;  { Uppercase }
278
279   {*******************************************************************}
280
281   procedure Initialize;
282
283      {-----------------------------------------------------------------}
284      {  Initialize is called once at the beginning of the program.    }
285      {  It assigns external names for the files CRYPTO and CCOUNT, if  }
286      {  this is required in the version of Pascal being used.  It also }
287      {  clears the terminal screen.                                    }
288      {-----------------------------------------------------------------}
289
290     begin  { Initialize }
291
292        { ## Non-standard statements -- Turbo Pascal version }
293
294        assign(CRYPTO,'CRYPTO');
295        assign(CCOUNT,'CCOUNT');
296
297        { End Turbo Pascal version }
298
299        ClearScreen
300
301     end;  { Initialize }
302
303   {*******************************************************************}
304
305   procedure GetCipher(var Cryptogram : CryptoPuzzle);
306
307      {-----------------------------------------------------------------}
308      {  GetCipher is called to read a cryptogram to be solved from      }
```

```
309   { the file CRYPTO.  It first calls an internal procedure       }
310   { FindNextCipher to locate the next cryptogram to be processed. }
311   { Then it reads the cryptogram, stores the ciphertext and the   }
312   { deciphering key in the record Cryptogram, and initializes the }
313   { remaining fields in Cryptogram.                               }
314   {                                                               }
315   { If the ciphertext consists of more than one line, end-of-line }
316   { is indicated in Cryptogram.Ciphertext with the character '&'. }
317   {                                                               }
318   { Input parameters: None                                        }
319   {                                                               }
320   { Output parameters:                                            }
321   {    Cryptogram - the cryptogram to be solved                   }
322   {---------------------------------------------------------------}
323
324   var
325      Letter : char;              { used as subscript for CipherKey }
326      I : integer;               { used as subscript for Ciphertext }
327      CharacterCount : integer;   { count of characters in Ciphertext }
328      Character : char;           { current ciphertext character }
329
330   {+++++++++++++++++++++++++++++++++++++++++++++++++++++++++++++++++}
331
332   procedure FindNextCipher;
333
334      {---------------------------------------------------------------}
335      { FindNextCipher is called at the beginning of GetCipher to locate }
336      { the next cryptogram in CRYPTO to be processed.  It reads the   }
337      { file CCOUNT, obtaining the number of the last cryptogram that  }
338      { was processed and the total number of cryptograms in CRYPTO.   }
339      { The cryptogram to be processed is the one following the one    }
340      { last processed, or the first one in CRYPTO if the last one was }
341      { just processed.                                               }
342      {                                                               }
343      { After determining the number of the cryptogram to be processed, }
344      { FindNextCipher updates the file CCOUNT.  It then reads the file }
345      { CRYPTO, skipping cryptograms until the beginning of the one to }
346      { be processed is reached.                                      }
347      {                                                               }
348      { Input parameters: None                                        }
349      {                                                               }
350      { Output parameters: None                                       }
351      {                                                               }
352      { Side effect:  The file CRYPTO is positioned to the beginning  }
353      {               of the cryptogram to be processed.             }
354      {---------------------------------------------------------------}
355
356   var
357      PreviousCipherNumber : integer;    { cryptogram previously processed }
358      LastCipherNumber : integer;        { number of cryptograms in CRYPTO }
359      CurrentCipherNumber : integer;     { cryptogram to process this time }
360      CipherCount : integer;             { count of cryptograms skipped }
361      Flag : char;                       { character read from CRYPTO }
```

```
362
363     begin  { FindNextCipher }
364
365       { read CCOUNT and determine next cryptogram to process }
366
367       reset(CCOUNT);
368       readln(CCOUNT,PreviousCipherNumber,LastCipherNumber);
369       if PreviousCipherNumber < LastCipherNumber then
370         CurrentCipherNumber := PreviousCipherNumber + 1
371       else
372         CurrentCipherNumber := 1;
373
374       { update CCOUNT to reflect cryptogram being processed }
375
376       rewrite(CCOUNT);
377       writeln(CCOUNT,CurrentCipherNumber:6,LastCipherNumber:6);
378
379       { read CRYPTO, skipping cryptograms until the beginning of the one
380         to be processed.  the end of each cryptogram in CRYPTO is marked
381         by a line containing the character '#'. }
382
383       reset(CRYPTO);
384       CipherCount := 1;
385       while CipherCount < CurrentCipherNumber do
386         begin
387           readln(CRYPTO,Flag);
388           if Flag = '#' then CipherCount := CipherCount + 1
389         end   { while }
390
391     end;  { FindNextCipher }
392
393   {++++++++++++++++++++++++++++++++++++++++++++++++++++++++++++++++++++++}
394
395     begin   { GetCipher }
396
397       { find the cryptogram to be processed }
398
399       FindNextCipher;
400
401       { read the deciphering key }
402
403       for Letter := 'a' to 'z' do
404         read(CRYPTO,Cryptogram.CipherKey[Letter]);
405       readln(CRYPTO);
406
407       { read the ciphertext from CRYPTO, counting the characters and storing
408         them in Cryptogram.Ciphertext }
409
410       read(CRYPTO,Character);
411       CharacterCount := 0;
412       while Character <> '#' do
413         begin
414           CharacterCount := CharacterCount + 1;
```

```
415        Cryptogram.Ciphertext[CharacterCount] := Character;
416        if eoln(CRYPTO) then
417
418           { represent end-of-line in Ciphertext with the character '&' }
419
420           begin
421             CharacterCount := CharacterCount + 1;
422             Cryptogram.Ciphertext[CharacterCount] := '&';
423             readln(CRYPTO)
424           end;   { if eoln }
425
426         read(CRYPTO,Character)
427       end;   { while }
428
429     { store length of ciphertext and set "cryptogram solved" flag to false }
430
431     Cryptogram.CipherLength := CharacterCount;
432     Cryptogram.Solved := false;
433
434     { copy non-alphabetic characters in ciphertext to the working plaintext;
435       initialize all other plaintext characters to blank }
436
437     for I := 1 to Cryptogram.CipherLength do
438       if Cryptogram.Ciphertext[I] in ['a'..'z'] then
439         Cryptogram.Plaintext[I] := ' '
440       else
441         Cryptogram.Plaintext[I] := Cryptogram.Ciphertext[I]
442
443   end;   { GetCipher }
444
445 {*********************************************************************}
446
447 procedure CountFrequencies(var Cryptogram : CryptoPuzzle);
448
449     {-------------------------------------------------------------------}
450     {  CountFrequencies is called to determine the most frequently      }
451     {  occurring letters in a cryptogram and to enter these letters     }
452     {  with their frequencies in Cryptogram.CommonLetters.  It uses an  }
453     {  internal procedure CountCharacters to count the number of        }
454     {  occurrences of each letter in the ciphertext, and another        }
455     {  internal procedure BuildSortedList to sort the letters by        }
456     {  number of occurrences.  It then calculates the relative          }
457     {  frequency of the eight most common letters, and enters this      }
458     {  information in Cryptogram.CommonLetters.                         }
459     {                                                                   }
460     {  Input parameters:                                                }
461     {    Cryptogram - the cryptogram being processed by the program     }
462     {                                                                   }
463     {  Output parameters:                                              }
464     {    Cryptogram - the input cryptogram, with common letters and     }
465     {                 letter frequencies                               }
466     {-------------------------------------------------------------------}
467
```

```
468      type
469        CountOfLetters = array['a'..'z'] of integer;
470        LetterStats = record              { entry in table used for sorting }
471                        Letter : char;     { letter of the alphabet }
472                        Count : integer     { count of occurrences of that letter }
473                      end;
474        ListOfCounts = array [1..26] of LetterStats;
475
476      var
477        LetterCounts : CountOfLetters;     { count of occurrences for each letter }
478        SortedList : ListOfCounts;          { table used for sorting by count }
479        TotalLetters : integer;             { total number of letters counted }
480        I : integer;                        { used as subscript for CommonLetters }
481
482    {++++++++++++++++++++++++++++++++++++++++++++++++++++++++++++++++++++++++}
483
484    procedure CountCharacters(Cryptogram : CryptoPuzzle;
485                var LetterCounts : CountOfLetters; var TotalLetters : integer);
486
487      {---------------------------------------------------------------------}
488      {   CountCharacters scans the characters in Cryptogram.Ciphertext,    }
489      {   one character at a time.  It counts the alphabetic characters     }
490      {   found, using the array LetterCounts.  The total number of         }
491      {   letters counted is stored in TotalLetters.  All letters in the    }
492      {   ciphertext are assumed to be in lower case.                       }
493      {                                                                     }
494      {   The array LetterCounts and the variable TotalLetters are          }
495      {   initialized to zero before the counting begins.                   }
496      {                                                                     }
497      {   The counting of letters in this procedure is essentially similar }
498      {   to that performed by the procedure CountCharacters in program     }
499      {   Letters1.  The main difference is that this version takes the      }
500      {   letters to be counted from Cryptogram.Ciphertext, whereas the     }
501      {   version in Letters1 reads the characters from a data file.         }
502      {                                                                     }
503      {   Input parameters:                                                 }
504      {     Cryptogram - the cryptogram whose characters are to be counted }
505      {                                                                     }
506      {   Output parameters:                                                }
507      {     LetterCounts - counts of each alphabetic character in           }
508      {                       Cryptogram.Ciphertext                         }
509      {     TotalLetters - the total number of letters counted              }
510      {---------------------------------------------------------------------}
511
512      var
513        Character : char;      { character from ciphertext }
514        I : integer;           { used as subscript for Cryptogram.Ciphertext }
515        Letter : char;         { used as subscript for LetterCounts }
516
517      begin  { CountCharacters }
518
519        { initialize letter counts and total letters to zero }
520
```

```
521        for Character := 'a' to 'z' do
522          LetterCounts[Character] := 0;
523        TotalLetters := 0;
524
525        { scan the characters in Cryptogram.Ciphertext }
526
527        for I := 1 to Cryptogram.CipherLength do
528          begin
529            Character := Cryptogram.Ciphertext[I];
530
531            { if the character is 'a' through 'z', add one to the
532              corresponding count in LetterCounts }
533
534            if Character in ['a'..'z'] then
535              LetterCounts[Character] := LetterCounts[Character] + 1
536          end;  { for }
537
538        { calculate the total number of letters counted }
539
540        for Letter := 'a' to 'z' do
541          TotalLetters := TotalLetters + LetterCounts[Letter]
542
543      end;  { CountCharacters }
544
545  {++++++++++++++++++++++++++++++++++++++++++++++++++++++++++++++++++++++++}
546
547  procedure BuildSortedList (LetterCounts : CountOfLetters;
548                             var LetterList : ListOfCounts);
549
550      {--------------------------------------------------------------------}
551      {  BuildSortedList inserts each letter and the number of occurrences}
552      {  of that letter into the array LetterList.  The entries in        }
553      {  LetterList are then sorted by number of occurrences, using a     }
554      {  simple exchange sort.                                            }
555      {                                                                   }
556      {  Input parameters:                                                }
557      {     LetterCounts - number of occurrences of each letter           }
558      {                                                                   }
559      {  Output parameters:                                               }
560      {     LetterList - list of letters and number of occurrences, sorted }
561      {                  by number of occurrences                         }
562      {--------------------------------------------------------------------}
563
564      var
565        Character : char;        { used as subscript for LetterCounts }
566        I : integer;             { used as subscript for LetterList }
567        Start : integer;         { working variables used in exchange sort }
568        Compare : integer;
569        Hold : LetterStats;
570
571      begin  { BuildSortedList }
572
573        { enter each letter and its number of occurrences into LetterList.
```

```
574            Character is used as a subscript for LetterCounts, I as a subscript
575            for LetterList }
576
577          Character := 'a';
578          for I := 1 to 26 do
579            begin
580              LetterList[I].Letter := Character;
581              LetterList[I].Count := LetterCounts[Character];
582              Character := succ(Character)
583            end;
584
585          { sort the entries in LetterList by number of occurrences }
586
587          for Start := 1 to 25 do
588            for Compare := Start+1 to 26 do
589
590              { Start and Compare are subscripts indicating entries in
591                LetterList, with Start preceding Compare in the array. }
592
593              if LetterList[Start].Count < LetterList[Compare].Count then
594                begin
595
596                  { if the number of occurrences in entry Start is less then
597                    the number of occurrences in entry Compare, exchange these
598                    two entries. }
599
600                  Hold := LetterList[Start];
601                  LetterList[Start] := LetterList[Compare];
602                  LetterList[Compare] := Hold
603                end
604
605      end;  { BuildSortedList }
606
607  {++++++++++++++++++++++++++++++++++++++++++++++++++++++++++++++++++++++++}
608
609      begin  { CountFrequencies }
610
611        { count characters in ciphertext and build list sorted by number
612          of occurrences }
613
614        CountCharacters(Cryptogram,LetterCounts,TotalLetters);
615        BuildSortedList(LetterCounts,SortedList);
616
617        { insert the eight most common letters, with their frequencies,
618          into Cryptogram.CommonLetters }
619
620        for I := 1 to 8 do
621          begin
622            Cryptogram.CommonLetters[I].Letter := SortedList[I].Letter;
623            Cryptogram.CommonLetters[I].Frequency :=
624                        SortedList[I].Count / TotalLetters
625          end  { for }
626
```

```
627     end;   { CountFrequencies }
628
629   {*********************************************************************}
630
631   procedure DisplayCiphertext(Cryptogram : CryptoPuzzle);
632
633     {-------------------------------------------------------------------}
634     {  DisplayCiphertext is called once, after the cryptogram has been  }
635     {  read and its letter frequencies calculated.  It displays the     }
636     {  ciphertext on the terminal, beginning on line 2 of the screen.   }
637     {  If the ciphertext consists of more than one line, the succeeding }
638     {  lines are displayed on lines 5, 8, 11 and 14 of the screen.      }
639     {  (Space is left between the lines to allow for later display of   }
640     {  plaintext decipherments with each line of ciphertext.)  The      }
641     {  eight most common ciphertext letters, with their frequencies,    }
642     {  are displayed on line 17 of the screen; the eight most common    }
643     {  English letters are displayed for reference on line 18.          }
644     {                                                                   }
645     {  Input parameters:                                                }
646     {    Cryptogram - the cryptogram whose ciphertext and letter        }
647     {                      frequencies are to be displayed              }
648     {                                                                   }
649     {  Output parameters: None                                          }
650     {-------------------------------------------------------------------}
651
652     var
653       I : integer;              { used as subscript for Cryptogram.Ciphertext }
654       LineNumber : integer;     { current line number on the terminal screen }
655       Percentage : integer;     { letter frequency, expressed as a percentage }
656
657     begin   { DisplayCiphertext }
658
659       { move cursor to the beginning of line 2 on the screen }
660
661       LineNumber := 2;
662       MoveCursor(LineNumber,1);
663
664       { scan the ciphertext, writing each character to the screen.  if the
665         character '&' (indicating end-of-line) is found, move to the start
666         of the third line below the current cursor position }
667
668       for I := 1 to Cryptogram.CipherLength do
669         if Cryptogram.Ciphertext[I] = '&' then
670           begin
671             LineNumber := LineNumber + 3;
672             MoveCursor(LineNumber,1)
673           end   { if & }
674         else
675           write(Cryptogram.Ciphertext[I]);
676       writeln;
677
678       { move to line 17 and write list of common letters in ciphertext }
679
```

```
680          MoveCursor(17,1);
681          write('In ciphertext:');
682          for I := 1 to 8 do
683            begin
684
685              { express each frequency as a percentage, to the nearest whole percent }
686
687              Percentage := round(100 * Cryptogram.CommonLetters[I].Frequency);
688              write('   ',Cryptogram.CommonLetters[I].Letter,Percentage:3,'%')
689            end;
690          writeln;
691
692          { write list of common letters in English }
693
694          write('In English:     E 13%   T  9%   A  8%   O  8%   N  7%   ');
695          writeln('I  7%   R  7%   S  7%')
696
697       end;  { DisplayCiphertext }
698
699   {*********************************************************************}
700
701   procedure DisplayPlaintext(Cryptogram : CryptoPuzzle);
702
703       {------------------------------------------------------------------}
704       {  DisplayPlaintext is called after each command is processed.     }
705       {  It displays the working decipherment from Cryptogram.Plaintext, }
706       {  positioning each character above the corresponding ciphertext   }
707       {  character.  In order to do this, it begins the display on line 1 }
708       {  of the terminal screen.  If the ciphertext consists of more than }
709       {  one line, the succeeding lines of plaintext are displayed on     }
710       {  lines 4, 7, 10 and 13 of the screen.                            }
711       {                                                                  }
712       {  Input parameters:                                               }
713       {    Cryptogram - the cryptogram whose working plaintext is to be  }
714       {                 displayed                                        }
715       {                                                                  }
716       {  Output parameters: None                                         }
717       {------------------------------------------------------------------}
718
719   var
720       I : integer;                    { used as subscript for Cryptogram.Plaintext }
721       LineNumber : integer;           { current line number on the terminal screen }
722
723   begin  { DisplayPlaintext }
724       LineNumber := 1;
725       MoveCursor(LineNumber,1);
726
727       { scan the plaintext, writing each character to the screen.  if the
728         character '&' (indicating end-of-line) is found, move to the start
729         of the third line below the current cursor position }
730
731       for I := 1 to Cryptogram.CipherLength do
732         if Cryptogram.Plaintext[I] = '&' then
```

```
733             begin
734                LineNumber := LineNumber + 3;
735                MoveCursor(LineNumber,1)
736             end   { if & }
737           else
738             write(Cryptogram.Plaintext[I]);
739        writeln
740
741     end;   { DisplayPlaintext }
742
743   {**********************************************************************}
744
745   procedure GetCommand(var Command : CommandInfo);
746
747      {----------------------------------------------------------------------}
748      { GetCommand is called each time a new command is to be read from  }
749      { the terminal.  It uses an internal procedure ReadCommandLine     }
750      { to prompt the user for a command and to read the command line    }
751      { entered by the user.  It uses another internal procedure         }
752      { CheckCommand to test whether or not the command is valid.        }
753      { If the command is not valid, the terminal bell is sounded as     }
754      { an error indication.  This prompting and testing is repeated     }
755      { until a valid command is obtained.                               }
756      {                                                                  }
757      { Input parameters: None                                          }
758      {                                                                  }
759      { Output parameters:                                              }
760      {    Command - the valid command and parameters obtained           }
761      {----------------------------------------------------------------------}
762
763      var
764         CommandIsCorrect : boolean;      { command is valid }
765         Bell : char;                     { character to sound terminal bell }
766
767   {+++++++++++++++++++++++++++++++++++++++++++++++++++++++++++++++++++++++}
768
769      procedure ReadCommandLine(var Command : CommandInfo);
770
771         {----------------------------------------------------------------------}
772         { ReadCommandLine is called to prompt the user for a command and   }
773         { to read the command line entered in response to the  prompt.     }
774         { A maximum of five characters are read from the terminal (the     }
775         { longest valid command consists of five characters).  The first   }
776         { character entered is taken to be the command code.  The third    }
777         { character is taken to be the first parameter for the command     }
778         { (the parameter 'x' in commands  H x , B x , and  S x=y ).  The   }
779         { fifth character is taken to be the second parameter for the      }
780         { command (the parameter 'y' in command  S x=y ).  If fewer than   }
781         { five characters are entered on the command line, the unentered   }
782         { characters are considered as blanks.                             }
783         {                                                                  }
784         { The command code and second parameter are converted to upper     }
785         { case, and the first parameter is converted to lower case.  The   }
```

```
786      {   converted command code and parameters are returned in the      }
787      {   procedure parameter Command.                                   }
788      {                                                                  }
789      {   Input parameters: None                                        }
790      {                                                                  }
791      {   Output parameters:                                            }
792      {      Command - the command code and parameters read             }
793      {------------------------------------------------------------------}
794
795        var
796           CommandLine : array[1..5] of char;  { the input from the terminal }
797           I : integer;                         { used as subscript for CommandLine }
798
799        begin  { ReadCommandLine }
800
801           { move to line 21 on the terminal screen and prompt for a command }
802
803           MoveCursor(21,1);
804           ClearLine;
805           write('Enter command: ');
806
807           { read up to five characters.  if end-of-line is found before five
808             characters are read, fill the unread characters with blanks }
809
810           for I := 1 to 5 do
811             if eoln(input) then
812               CommandLine[I] := ' '
813             else
814               read(CommandLine[I]);
815           readln;
816
817           { convert cases and store command and parameters }
818
819           Command.CommandCode := Uppercase(CommandLine[1]);
820           Command.Parameter1 := Lowercase(CommandLine[3]);
821           Command.Parameter2 := Uppercase(CommandLine[5])
822
823        end;  { ReadCommandLine }
824
825   {+++++++++++++++++++++++++++++++++++++++++++++++++++++++++++++++++++++++++}
826
827     procedure CheckCommand(Command : CommandInfo; var CommandIsCorrect : boolean);
828
829        {------------------------------------------------------------------}
830        {  CheckCommand is called after a command line has been read.      }
831        {  It checks whether or not the command code and command parameters }
832        {  are valid, and sets the Boolean variable CommandIsCorrect        }
833        {  accordingly.                                                    }
834        {                                                                  }
835        {  Input parameters:                                              }
836        {     Command - the command code and parameters to be checked      }
837        {                                                                  }
838        {  Output parameters:                                             }
```

```
839        {      CommandIsCorrect - the result of the check                        }
840        {--------------------------------------------------------------------}
841
842          begin  { CheckCommand }
843
844             { command is assumed invalid until it is found to be correct }
845
846             CommandIsCorrect := false;
847
848             { if the command code is valid, check the parameters for the command }
849
850             if Command.CommandCode in ['B','H','S','Q'] then
851               case Command.CommandCode of
852                 'Q'     : if (Command.Parameter1 = ' ')
853                              and (Command.Parameter2 = ' ')
854                                 then CommandIsCorrect := true;
855                 'B','H' : if (Command.Parameter1 in ['a'..'z'])
856                              and (Command.Parameter2 = ' ')
857                                 then CommandIsCorrect := true;
858                 'S'     : if (Command.Parameter1 in ['a'..'z'])
859                              and (Command.Parameter2 in ['A'..'Z'])
860                                 then CommandIsCorrect := true
861                 end  { case }
862
863          end;  { CheckCommand }
864
865     {+++++++++++++++++++++++++++++++++++++++++++++++++++++++++++++++++++++++++}
866
867        begin  { GetCommand }
868
869             { if ASCII codes are being used, the character with ordinal value 7
870               causes the terminal bell to sound }
871
872             Bell := chr(7);
873
874             { move to line 20 and display a summary of the possible commands }
875
876             MoveCursor(20,1);
877             writeln('Commands are  S x=y , H x , B x , Q ');
878
879             { read and check command lines until a valid command is obtained.
880               sound the terminal bell if an invalid command is detected. }
881
882             repeat
883               ReadCommandLine(Command);
884               CheckCommand(Command,CommandIsCorrect);
885               if not CommandIsCorrect then
886                  write(Bell)
887             until CommandIsCorrect
888
889          end;  { GetCommand }
890
891     {*********************************************************************}
```

```
892
893     procedure ProcessCommand(Command : CommandInfo; var Cryptogram : CryptoPuzzle);
894
895        {-------------------------------------------------------------------}
896        {  ProcessCommand is called to control the processing of each       }
897        {  command entered by the user.  An internal procedure Substitute   }
898        {  is used to insert a given plaintext character in positions        }
899        {  that correspond to a given ciphertext character.  (The selection }
900        {  of the plaintext and ciphertext characters depends upon the      }
901        {  command being processed.)  After substitutions are performed,    }
902        {  another internal procedure CheckSolved is used to test whether   }
903        {  or not the cryptogram has been completely solved.                }
904        {                                                                   }
905        {  Input parameters:                                                }
906        {     Command - the command to be processed                         }
907        {     Cryptogram - the cryptogram being solved                      }
908        {                                                                   }
909        {  Output parameters:                                               }
910        {     Cryptogram - with Plaintext updated to reflect the effect of  }
911        {                  the command and Solved set to indicate whether   }
912        {                  , the solution is complete                       }
913        {-------------------------------------------------------------------}
914
915     var
916        Letter : char;              { used as subscript for CipherKey }
917        DecipheredLetter : char;    { the correct decipherment for a letter }
918
919   {+++++++++++++++++++++++++++++++++++++++++++++++++++++++++++++++++++++++++}
920
921     procedure Substitute(var Cryptogram : CryptoPuzzle; CipherCharacter : char;
922                          PlainCharacter : char);
923
924        {-------------------------------------------------------------------}
925        {  Substitute inserts PlainCharacter into the plaintext in all       }
926        {  positions where CipherCharacter occurs in the ciphertext.  It is }
927        {  used (in various ways) during the processing of all commands.    }
928        {                                                                   }
929        {  Input parameters:                                                }
930        {    Cryptogram - the cryptogram being solved                       }
931        {    PlainCharacter - the plaintext character to be substituted     }
932        {    CipherCharacter - the ciphertext character being substituted   }
933        {                      for                                          }
934        {                                                                   }
935        {  Output parameters:                                               }
936        {    Cryptogram - with Plaintext modified by the substitution       }
937        {-------------------------------------------------------------------}
938
939      var
940        I : integer;               { used as subscript for Ciphertext and Plaintext }
941
942      begin  { Substitute }
943
944        for I := 1 to Cryptogram.CipherLength do
```

```
945              if Cryptogram.Ciphertext[I] = CipherCharacter then
946                 Cryptogram.Plaintext[I] := PlainCharacter
947
948        end;  { Substitute }
949
950  {++++++++++++++++++++++++++++++++++++++++++++++++++++++++++++++++++++}
951
952    procedure CheckSolved(var Cryptogram : CryptoPuzzle);
953
954     {------------------------------------------------------------------}
955     {  CheckSolved is called after each substitution to check whether  }
956     {  or not the cryptogram is completely solved.  It scans the       }
957     {  plaintext and ciphertext, checking whether each plaintext       }
958     {  character is the correct decipherment of the corresponding      }
959     {  ciphertext character.  (Cryptogram.CipherKey gives the correct  }
960     {  decipherment for each ciphertext character.)  If any incorrect  }
961     {  decipherment is found, the scan is stopped and Cryptogram.Solved }
962     {  is set to false; if no errors are found, Cryptogram.Solved is   }
963     {  set to true.                                                    }
964     {                                                                  }
965     {  Input parameters:                                               }
966     {    Cryptogram - the cryptogram to be tested for solution         }
967     {                                                                  }
968     {  Output parameters:                                              }
969     {    Cryptogram - with Solved set to indicate whether the solution }
970     {                    is correct                                    }
971     {------------------------------------------------------------------}
972
973     var
974        I : integer;                  { subscript for Ciphertext and Plaintext }
975        NoErrorsFound : boolean;      { ciphertext and plaintext match so far }
976        CipherCharacter : char;       { character from ciphertext }
977        Decipherment : char;          { correct decipherment of CipherCharacter }
978
979     begin  { CheckSolved }
980
981        { scan ciphertext and plaintext until an error is found or the end
982          of the ciphertext is reached }
983
984        I := 1;
985        NoErrorsFound := true;
986        while (NoErrorsFound) and (I < Cryptogram.CipherLength) do
987          begin
988            CipherCharacter := Cryptogram.Ciphertext[I];
989
990            { if the current ciphertext character is alphabetic, get the
991              correct decipherment of it from CipherKey.  check whether the
992              corresponding plaintext character is correct. }
993
994            if CipherCharacter in ['a'..'z'] then
995              begin
996                Decipherment := Cryptogram.CipherKey[CipherCharacter];
997                if Cryptogram.Plaintext[I] <> Decipherment then
```

```
998                         NoErrorsFound := false
999                      end;
1000                  I := I + 1
1001                end;   { while }
1002
1003          { if no errors were found, the cryptogram is correctly solved }
1004
1005          Cryptogram.Solved := NoErrorsFound
1006
1007        end;   { CheckSolved }
1008
1009    {+++++++++++++++++++++++++++++++++++++++++++++++++++++++++++++++++++++++++}
1010
1011      begin   { ProcessCommand }
1012
1013        case Command.CommandCode of
1014
1015          'B' : { command is  B x -- substitute blanks for 'x' }
1016
1017                  Substitute(Cryptogram,Command.Parameter1,' ');
1018
1019          'S' : { command is  S x=y -- substitute 'y' for 'x' }
1020
1021                  begin  { 'S' }
1022                    Substitute(Cryptogram,Command.Parameter1,Command.Parameter2);
1023                    CheckSolved(Cryptogram)
1024                  end;   { 'S' }
1025
1026          'H' : { command is H x -- obtain the correct decipherment for 'x'
1027                  and substitute it for 'x' }
1028
1029                  begin  { 'H' }
1030                    DecipheredLetter := Cryptogram.CipherKey[Command.Parameter1];
1031                    Substitute(Cryptogram,Command.Parameter1,DecipheredLetter);
1032                    CheckSolved(Cryptogram)
1033                  end;   { 'H' }
1034
1035          'Q' : { command is Q -- substitute the correct decipherment for all
1036                  ciphertext characters }
1037
1038                  begin  { 'Q' }
1039                  for Letter := 'a' to 'z' do
1040                    begin
1041                      DecipheredLetter := Cryptogram.CipherKey[Letter];
1042                      Substitute(Cryptogram,Letter,DecipheredLetter)
1043                    end;   { for }
1044                  Cryptogram.Solved := true
1045                  end  { 'Q' }
1046
1047        end   { case }
1048
1049      end;   { ProcessCommand }
1050
```

```
1051      {*********************************************************************}
1052
1053      procedure CleanUp;
1054
1055         {---------------------------------------------------------------------}
1056         {  CleanUp is called once at the end of the program.  It closes      }
1057         {  the files CRYPTO and CCOUNT, if this is required in the Pascal    }
1058         {  version being used.  It also moves the cursor to line 22 on       }
1059         {  the screen, and waits for the user to enter a carriage return     }
1060         {  before exiting the program.                                       }
1061         {---------------------------------------------------------------------}
1062
1063         begin  { CleanUp }
1064
1065            { ## Non-standard statements -- Turbo Pascal version }
1066
1067            close(CRYPTO);
1068            close(CCOUNT);
1069
1070            { End Turbo Pascal version }
1071
1072            MoveCursor(22,1);
1073            ClearLine;
1074            write('Cryptogram solved -- press return to exit program');
1075            readln
1076
1077         end;  { CleanUp }
1078
1079      {*********************************************************************}
1080
1081      begin  { main program }
1082
1083         Initialize;
1084
1085         { read the cryptogram to be solved, count the frequencies of ciphertext
1086           characters, and display the ciphertext on the screen }
1087
1088         GetCipher(Cryptogram);
1089         CountFrequencies(Cryptogram);
1090         DisplayCiphertext(Cryptogram);
1091
1092         { read and process commands until the cryptogram is solved.  after each
1093           command is processed, display the partial plaintext solution }
1094
1095         while not Cryptogram.Solved do
1096           begin
1097             GetCommand(Command);
1098             ProcessCommand(Command,Cryptogram);
1099             DisplayPlaintext(Cryptogram)
1100           end;  { while }
1101
```

```
1102      CleanUp
1103
1104      end.
```

INCLUDE FILE

cases.i

```
1    {*************************************************************}
2
3    function Lowercase(Letter : char) : char;
4
5       {-------------------------------------------------------------}
6       {  Lowercase is used to convert alphabetic characters to lower }
7       {  case.  If the input parameter is an upper case letter       }
8       {  ('A' through 'Z'), the value of the function is the corresponding}
9       {  lower case letter ('a' through 'z').  If the input parameter is }
10      {  any other character, the value of the function is equal to the }
11      {  input parameter.                                            }
12      {                                                             }
13      {  Input parameters:                                          }
14      {     Letter - character to be converted to lower case         }
15      {                                                             }
16      {  Output parameters : None                                   }
17      {                                                             }
18      {  Function value : the value of the input parameter Letter,   }
19      {                   converted to lower case if it was originally }
20      {                   in the range 'A' through 'Z'              }
21      {-------------------------------------------------------------}
22
23      var
24         ConvertedLetter : char;        { the function value being computed }
25         DistancePastA : integer;       { the distance in the alphabet between
26                                          the letter being converted and 'A' }
27      begin  { Lowercase }
28
29         { if the input parameter is an upper case letter, convert it to
30           the corresponding lower case letter.  otherwise, the converted
31           letter is set equal to the input parameter. }
32
33         if Letter in ['A'..'Z'] then
34            begin
35               DistancePastA := ord(Letter) - ord('A');
36               ConvertedLetter := chr(ord('a') + DistancePastA)
37            end  { if }
38         else
39            ConvertedLetter := Letter;
40
41         { set the function value }
42
43         Lowercase := ConvertedLetter
```

131

```
44
45      end;  { Lowercase }
46
47   {***********************************************************************}
48
49   function Uppercase(Letter : char) : char;
50
51      {------------------------------------------------------------------}
52      {   Uppercase is used to convert alphabetic characters to upper     }
53      {   case.  If the input parameter is a lower case letter            }
54      {   ('a' through 'z'), the value of the function is the corresponding}
55      {   upper case letter ('A' through 'Z').  If the input parameter is  }
56      {   any other character, the value of the function is equal to the   }
57      {   input parameter.                                                 }
58      {                                                                    }
59      {   Input parameters:                                                }
60      {     Letter - character to be converted to upper case              }
61      {                                                                    }
62      {   Output parameters : None                                        }
63      {                                                                    }
64      {   Function value : the value of the input parameter Letter,        }
65      {                    converted to upper case if it was originally    }
66      {                    in the range 'a' through 'z'                    }
67      {------------------------------------------------------------------}
68
69   var
70      ConvertedLetter : char;        { the function value being computed }
71      DistancePastA : integer;       { the distance in the alphabet between
72                                       the letter being converted and 'a' }
73   begin  { Uppercase }
74
75      { if the input parameter is a lower case letter, convert it to
76        the corresponding upper case letter.  otherwise, the converted
77        letter is set equal to the input parameter. }
78
79      if Letter in ['a'..'z'] then
80        begin
81          DistancePastA := ord(Letter) - ord('a');
82          ConvertedLetter := chr(ord('A') + DistancePastA)
83        end  { if }
84      else
85        ConvertedLetter := Letter;
86
87      { set the function value }
88
89      Uppercase := ConvertedLetter
90
91   end;  { Uppercase }
```

INCLUDE FILE

display.i

```
 1   procedure Display(var Cells : CellArray; var OldCells : CellArray;
 2                     StartLine : integer);
 3
 4   {---------------------------------------------------------------------}
 5   {  Display displays the contents of the array Cells on the            }
 6   {  terminal, one row per line of the screen.  The first row of        }
 7   {  cells begins on the line specified by the parameter StartLine.      }
 8   {                                                                     }
 9   {  After displaying the contents of Cells, this version of the        }
10   {  procedure delays further execution of the program by a specified   }
11   {  number of milliseconds.  This delay is introduced to adjust the    }
12   {  pace of the screen display on fast machines.  The number of        }
13   {  milliseconds of delay is specified by the constant DelayCount,     }
14   {  which can be changed to provide satisfactory operation on your     }
15   {  machine.  The delay is accomplished by calling the nonstandard     }
16   {  Turbo Pascal procedure Delay.                                      }
17   {                                                                     }
18   {  It is assumed that the contents of the array OldCells have         }
19   {  already been displayed, and that this display remains on the       }
20   {  terminal screen.  Display attempts to avoid re-displaying          }
21   {  cells that have not changed from the previous version.  It         }
22   {  does this by scanning each row of Cells, comparing the cell        }
23   {  contents to those stored in OldCells.                              }
24   {                                                                     }
25   {  If the contents of a cell have changed, an internal procedure      }
26   {  DisplaySegment is called to display a segment of the row that      }
27   {  begins with the changed cell.  The scan then continues, skipping   }
28   {  over the segment that was displayed.                               }
29   {                                                                     }
30   {  Before Display is called for the first time, the terminal screen  }
31   {  should be cleared to blanks, and OldCells should be initialized    }
32   {  to blanks.  This insures that the first version of the array       }
33   {  will be correctly displayed.                                       }
34   {                                                                     }
35   {  Input parameters:                                                  }
36   {    Cells - the array whose contents are to be displayed             }
37   {    OldCells - the previous version of the array, or blanks if       }
38   {               this is the first call to Display                     }
39   {     Note: Cells and OldCells are var parameters for efficiency      }
40   {              in parameter passing.                                  }
41   {    StartLine - the line on the screen where the display of Cells    }
42   {               is to begin                                           }
43   {                                                                     }
```

```
44    {  Output parameters: None                                          }
45    {                                                                    }
46    {  In order to use this procedure, the main program must contain     }
47    {  the following constant and type definitions.  Items enclosed      }
48    {  in <<...>> are to be supplied by the programmer.                  }
49    {                                                                    }
50    {    const                                                           }
51    {      CellRows = <<integer between 1 and 20>>;                      }
52    {      CellCols = <<integer between 1 and 79>>;                      }
53    {                                                                    }
54    {    type                                                            }
55    {      CellArray = array[1..CellRows,1..CellCols] of char;           }
56    {      RowSubscript = 1..CellRows;                                   }
57    {      ColSubscript = 1..CellCols;                                   }
58    {                                                                    }
59    {  In addition, the main program must include the terminal output    }
60    {  routines from the file "screen.i".                                }
61    {--------------------------------------------------------------------}
62
63    const
64      DelayCount = 250;                    { number of milliseconds to delay }
65
66    var
67      Row : RowSubscript;                  { Row and Col are used as subscripts }
68      Col : ColSubscript;                  {     for Cells and OldCells          }
69      Length : integer;                    { the length of the segment displayed }
70      EndOfRow : boolean;                  { the end of a row has been reached }
71
72    {+++++++++++++++++++++++++++++++++++++++++++++++++++++++++++++++++++++++++++++++}
73
74    procedure DisplaySegment(var Cells: CellArray; var OldCells : CellArray;
75                             Row : RowSubscript; Col : ColSubscript;
76                             var Length : integer; StartLine : integer);
77
78    {--------------------------------------------------------------------}
79    {  DisplaySegment is called each time Display finds a cell that       }
80    {  has changed in value from the previous version.  It scans the      }
81    {  row containing the changed cell to find the segment to be          }
82    {  displayed.  This scan begins with the changed cell and             }
83    {  continues until the end of the row is reached, or until six        }
84    {  consecutive unchanged cells are found in the row.                  }
85    {                                                                    }
86    {  (This rule for constructing the segment to display takes into      }
87    {  account a typical amount of overhead involved in moving the        }
88    {  the cursor to a new location.  On most terminals, it is more       }
89    {  efficient to display a small number of unchanged cells than to     }
90    {  reposition the cursor to skip over them.)                          }
91    {                                                                    }
92    {  The segment that is found is displayed on the terminal, after      }
93    {  moving the cursor to the proper starting location.  The length     }
94    {  of the segment displayed is returned to the calling procedure.     }
95    {                                                                    }
96    {  Input parameters:                                                  }
```

```
 97    {      Cells - the array whose contents are being displayed      }
 98    {      OldCells - the previous version of the array, or blanks if  }
 99    {            this is the first call to DisplaySegment             }
100    {      Note: Cells and OldCells are var parameters for efficiency }
101    {            in parameter passing.                                 }
102    {      Row,Col - the row and column in which a changed cell occurs }
103    {      StartLine - the line on the screen where the display of Cells}
104    {            begins                                                 }
105    {                                                                   }
106    {  Output parameters:                                              }
107    {      Length - the length of the segment displayed                }
108    {-------------------------------------------------------------------}
109
110      var
111         CurrentCol : ColSubscript;        { used as subscript for scanning the row }
112         LastChangedCol : ColSubscript;    { last changed cell found in the row }
113         UnchangedCells : integer;         { number of consecutive unchanged cells }
114         WriteCol : ColSubscript;          { used as subscript to display segment }
115         EndOfSegment : boolean;           { the end of the segment to display
116                                             has been found }
117
118      begin  { DisplaySegment }
119
120         { start scanning with the changed column passed as parameter }
121
122         LastChangedCol := Col;
123         CurrentCol := Col;
124         UnchangedCells := 0;
125         EndOfSegment := false;
126
127         { scan cells until the end of the row is reached, or until six
128           consecutive unchanged cells are found }
129
130         repeat  { until EndOfSegment }
131           if CurrentCol = CellCols then
132             EndOfSegment := true
133           else
134             begin
135
136               { not at end of row -- check whether next cell is changed }
137
138               CurrentCol := CurrentCol + 1;
139               if Cells[Row,CurrentCol] = OldCells[Row,CurrentCol] then
140                 begin
141
142                   { count unchanged cell; stop scanning if six unchanged
143                     cells have been found }
144
145                   UnchangedCells := UnchangedCells + 1;
146                   if UnchangedCells = 6 then
147                     EndOfSegment := true
148                 end  { if cell is unchanged }
149               else
```

```
150                     begin
151
152                        { remember where the changed cell was found and reset the
153                          count of consecutive unchanged cells to zero }
154
155                        LastChangedCol := CurrentCol;
156                        UnchangedCells := 0
157                     end  { else -- cell is changed }
158                  end  { else -- not at end of row }
159            until EndOfSegment;
160
161            { position cursor and display segment, ending with last changed cell
162              that was found }
163
164            MoveCursor(StartLine + Row - 1,Col);
165            for WriteCol := Col to LastChangedCol do
166              write(Cells[Row,WriteCol]);
167            writeln;
168
169            { set length of segment that was displayed }
170
171            Length := LastChangedCol - Col + 1
172
173         end;  { DisplaySegment }
174
175   {+++++++++++++++++++++++++++++++++++++++++++++++++++++++++++++++++++++++++}
176
177      begin  { Display }
178
179         { scan each row of the cell array, looking for a cell that has
180           changed from the previous generation }
181
182         for Row := 1 to CellRows do
183           begin
184             Col := 1;
185             EndOfRow := false;
186             repeat  { until EndOfRow }
187               if Cells[Row,Col] = OldCells[Row,Col] then
188                 begin
189
190                    { cell is unchanged -- go on to next cell, unless at end of row }
191
192                    if Col = CellCols then
193                      EndOfRow := true
194                    else
195                      Col := Col + 1
196
197                 end  { if cell is unchanged }
198               else
199                 begin
200
201                    { a changed cell was found -- display a segment starting with
202                      that cell and skip over the segment displayed }
```

```
203
204                  DisplaySegment(Cells,OldCells,Row,Col,Length,StartLine);
205                  if (Col + Length) > CellCols then
206                    EndOfRow := true
207                  else
208                    Col := Col + Length
209              end  { else -- cell is changed }
210          until EndOfRow
211        end;  { for }
212
213    { introduce a delay to adjust the pace of the display for fast machines }
214
215    { ## Non-standard statements -- Turbo Pascal version }
216
217      Delay(DelayCount)
218
219      { End Turbo Pascal version }
220
221    end;  { Display }
```

```
 1    {------------------------------------------------------------------}
 2    {  The following procedures and functions implement operations on the }
 3    {  abstract data type PhraseType.  This data type can be used to       }
 4    {  represent a phrase, which is a sequence of words separated by       }
 5    {  spaces.  The maximum number of characters in a word is given by     }
 6    {  the constant MaxWordLength.  The maximum number of characters in a  }
 7    {  phrase (including the spaces between words) is given by the         }
 8    {  constant MaxPhraseLength.  The following procedures and functions   }
 9    {  are provided:                                                       }
10    {                                                                      }
11    {     InitPhrase - initializes a phrase so that it contains no words   }
12    {     AddToPhrase - adds a new word at the end of a phrase             }
13    {     DisplayPhrase - displays a phrase on the terminal               }
14    {     WordsInPhrase - returns the current number of words in a phrase  }
15    {                                                                      }
16    {  In order to use this abstract data type, the main program must      }
17    {  contain the following constant and type definitions.  Items         }
18    {  enclosed in <<...>> are to be supplied by the programmer.           }
19    {                                                                      }
20    {    const                                                             }
21    {      MaxWordLength = << integer between 1 and 80 >>;                 }
22    {      MaxPhraseLength = << integer between 1 and 80 >>;               }
23    {                                                                      }
24    {    type                                                              }
25    {                                                                      }
26    {      WordArray = array[1..MaxWordLength] of char;                    }
27    {                                                                      }
28    {      PhraseType = record                                            }
29    {                      CharCount : 0..MaxPhraseLength;                }
30    {                      WordCount : integer;                          }
31    {                      Contents : array[1..MaxPhraseLength] of char  }
32    {                  end;                                               }
33    {                                                                      }
34    {  In this implementation of PhraseType, a phrase is represented by    }
35    {  a record that contains the following fields:                        }
36    {                                                                      }
37    {     CharCount - the number of characters currently in the phrase    }
38    {     WordCount - the number of words currently in the phrase         }
39    {     Contents - an array containing the characters in the phrase     }
40    {                                                                      }
41    {  The maximum number of characters allowed in a phrase is 80.         }
42    {                                                                      }
43    {  A word to be added to a phrase is represented as an (unpacked)      }
```

138

```
44    {  array of characters, with length given by the constant          }
45    {  MaxWordLength.                                                   }
46    {------------------------------------------------------------------}
47
48
49    {++++++++++++++++++++++++++++++++++++++++++++++++++++++++++++++++++}
50
51    procedure InitPhrase(var Phrase : PhraseType);
52
53       {---------------------------------------------------------------}
54       {  InitPhrase is called to initialize a phrase.  It sets the    }
55       {  contents of the phrase to all blanks, the length of the phrase }
56       {  to zero, and the number of words in the phrase to zero.      }
57       {                                                               }
58       {  Input parameters: None                                      }
59       {                                                               }
60       {  Output parameters:                                          }
61       {     Phrase - the initialized phrase                          }
62       {---------------------------------------------------------------}
63
64       var
65         I : integer;          { used as subscript for Contents }
66
67       begin  { InitPhrase }
68
69         for I := 1 to MaxPhraseLength do
70           Phrase.Contents[I] := ' ';
71         Phrase.CharCount := 0;
72         Phrase.WordCount := 0
73
74       end;  { InitPhrase }
75
76    {++++++++++++++++++++++++++++++++++++++++++++++++++++++++++++++++++}
77
78    procedure AddToPhrase(OldPhrase : PhraseType; NewWord : WordArray;
79                     WordLength : integer; var NewPhrase : PhraseType);
80
81       {---------------------------------------------------------------}
82       {  AddToPhrase adds a word to an existing phrase, creating a new }
83       {  phrase. If the new word will not fit in the existing phrase, }
84       {  an error message is displayed.                              }
85       {                                                               }
86       {  Input parameters:                                           }
87       {     OldPhrase - the existing phrase to which a word is to be added }
88       {     NewWord - the new word to add to the phrase              }
89       {     WordLength - the number of characters in NewWord         }
90       {                                                               }
91       {  Output parameters:                                          }
92       {     NewPhrase - the phrase with the new word added           }
93       {---------------------------------------------------------------}
94
95       var
96         I : integer;                   { used as subscript for Contents }
```

```
97           StartingPoint : integer;      { starting point in Contents for new word }
98
99       begin  { AddToPhrase }
100
101         { check to be sure that the new word will fit in the phrase }
102
103         if (OldPhrase.CharCount + WordLength) > MaxPhraseLength then
104           writeln('*** AddToPhrase: Word is too long to be added to phrase')
105         else
106           begin  { add the word to the phrase }
107
108             { copy the contents of the old phrase to the new phrase }
109
110             for I := 1 to MaxPhraseLength do
111               NewPhrase.Contents[I] := OldPhrase.Contents[I];
112
113             { start the new word after the end of the previous word(s) }
114
115             StartingPoint := OldPhrase.CharCount + 1;
116
117             { add the new word, setting the phrase length and the number of words }
118
119             for I := 1 to WordLength do
120               NewPhrase.Contents[StartingPoint + I] := NewWord[I];
121             NewPhrase.CharCount := OldPhrase.CharCount + WordLength + 1;
122             NewPhrase.WordCount := OldPhrase.WordCount + 1;
123
124           end  { adding word to the phrase }
125
126       end;  { AddToPhrase }
127
128   {++++++++++++++++++++++++++++++++++++++++++++++++++++++++++++++++++++++++}
129
130   procedure DisplayPhrase(Phrase : PhraseType);
131
132       {----------------------------------------------------------------------}
133       {  DisplayPhrase displays a phrase on the terminal.  The characters }
134       {  in the phrase are displayed, followed by a carriage return.        }
135       {                                                                     }
136       {  Input parameters:                                                  }
137       {     Phrase - the phrase to be displayed                             }
138       {                                                                     }
139       {  Output parameters: None                                           }
140       {----------------------------------------------------------------------}
141
142       var
143         I : integer;      { used as subscript for Phrase.Contents }
144
145       begin  { DisplayPhrase }
146
147         for I := 1 to Phrase.CharCount do
148           write(Phrase.Contents[I]);
149         writeln
```

```
150
151      end;   { DisplayPhrase }
152
153   {+++++++++++++++++++++++++++++++++++++++++++++++++++++++++++++++++++++++}
154
155   function WordsInPhrase(Phrase : PhraseType) : integer;
156
157      {-------------------------------------------------------------------}
158      {  WordsInPhrase returns the number of words currently in a phrase. }
159      {                                                                   }
160      {  Input parameters:                                                }
161      {     Phrase - the phrase to be processed                           }
162      {                                                                   }
163      {  Output parameters: None                                          }
164      {                                                                   }
165      {  Function value: the number of words in Phrase                    }
166      {-------------------------------------------------------------------}
167
168      begin   { WordsInPhrase }
169
170         WordsInPhrase := Phrase.WordCount
171
172      end;   { WordsInPhrase }
```

INCLUDE FILE
random.i

```
1     function RandomNumber : real;
2
3        {----------------------------------------------------------------------}
4        {   RandomNumber returns a random real number between 0 and 1.   The   }
5        {   random numbers generated are uniformly distributed in this         }
6        {   range.   Before calling RandomNumber, the random-number generator  }
7        {   should be initialized by a call to procedure InitRandom.           }
8        {                                                                      }
9        {   RandomNumber calls a non-standard Pascal library routine to        }
10       {   generate the random numbers required.                              }
11       {                                                                      }
12       {   Function value: a random real number between 0 and 1               }
13       {----------------------------------------------------------------------}
14
15    begin   { RandomNumber }
16
17        { ## Non-standard statements -- Turbo Pascal version }
18
19        RandomNumber := Random
20
21        { End Turbo Pascal version }
22
23        { ## Non-standard statements -- Berkeley Pascal version }
24        {
25        RandomNumber := random(1.0)
26        }
27        { End Berkeley Pascal version }
28
29    end;   { RandomNumber }
30
31   {**********************************************************************}
32
33   procedure InitRandom(SeedValue : integer);
34
35       {----------------------------------------------------------------------}
36       {   InitRandom initializes the random-number generator.   The          }
37       {   sequence of random numbers generated is determined by the          }
38       {   parameter SeedValue, if this value is not zero.   If SeedValue      }
39       {   is zero, the random-number generator is initialized with a         }
40       {   value derived from the system clock.   This causes a different     }
41       {   sequence of random numbers to be generated each time the program   }
42       {   is executed.   The procedure calls a non-standard Pascal library   }
43       {   routine to perform this operation.                                 }
```

```
44    {                                                                      }
45    {  Input parameters:                                                    }
46    {    SeedValue - a value to be used in initializing the random          }
47    {            number generator, or zero                                  }
48    {                                                                       }
49    {  Output parameters: none                                             }
50    {                                                                       }
51    {  Side effect:  The random number generator is initialized,           }
52    {                depending upon the value of SeedValue                 }
53    {-----------------------------------------------------------------}
54
55    var
56       Dummy : integer;          { a dummy variable required by the syntax of
57                                   Berkeley Pascal -- value is never used }
58
59    begin  { InitRandom }
60
61       { ## Non-standard statements -- Turbo Pascal version }
62
63       if SeedValue = 0 then
64         Randomize
65       else
66         RandSeed := SeedValue
67
68       { End Turbo Pascal version }
69
70       { ## Non-standard statements -- Berkeley Pascal version }
71       {
72       if SeedValue = 0 then
73         Dummy := seed(wallclock)
74       else
75         Dummy := seed(SeedValue)
76       }
77       { End Berkeley Pascal version }
78
79    end;   { InitRandom }
```

INCLUDE FILE
reclist.i

```
 1   {----------------------------------------------------------------------}
 2   {  The following procedures and function implement operations on        }
 3   {  the abstract data type ListOfRecords.  This data type can be used    }
 4   {  to store and retrieve a collection of records. The fields            }
 5   {  contained in these records can be defined by the programmer.         }
 6   {                                                                       }
 7   {  Procedures:                                                          }
 8   {    InitList - initialize a new (empty) list                           }
 9   {    GetFirst - get the first record (if any) in a list                 }
10   {    GetNext - get the next record (if any) in a list                   }
11   {    UpdateCurrent - update the last record read from a list            }
12   {    DeleteCurrent - delete the last record read from a list            }
13   {    AddNew - add a new record to a list                                }
14   {                                                                       }
15   {  Function:                                                            }
16   {    NumberIn - returns the number of records in a list                 }
17   {                                                                       }
18   {  The records in a list can be retrieved, one at a time, by using      }
19   {  the operations GetFirst and GetNext.  GetFirst begins a new scan     }
20   {  of the records in the list and retrieves the first record.  Each     }
21   {  record after the first is retrieved with GetNext.  When no more      }
22   {  records remain to be retrieved, the parameter EndOfList is set to    }
23   {  true.                                                                }
24   {                                                                       }
25   {  This sequence of operations is guaranteed to retrieve every record   }
26   {  in the list before terminating.  However, the order in which the     }
27   {  records are retrieved is not defined, and may vary from one scan      }
28   {  of the list to the next.                                             }
29   {                                                                       }
30   {  The record most recently retrieved is designated as the current      }
31   {  record of the list.  This record can be modified by using the        }
32   {  operation UpdateCurrent, or deleted from the list by using the       }
33   {  operation DeleteCurrent.  It is not possible to modify or delete      }
34   {  records other than the current record.                               }
35   {                                                                       }
36   {  New records can be added to the list at any time with the            }
37   {  operation AddNew.  If a new record is added during a scan of the     }
38   {  list, it will be retrieved later during that same scan.              }
39   {                                                                       }
40   {  In order to use these routines, the main program must contain the    }
41   {  following constant and type definitions.  Items enclosed in          }
42   {  <<...>> are to be supplied by the programmer.                        }
43   {                                                                       }
```

```
44  {    const                                                      }
45  {       MaximumListSize = << maximum size of a list >>          }
46  {                                                               }
47  {    type                                                       }
48  {       ListEntry = record                                      }
49  {                      << definitions of fields in a record >>  }
50  {                    end;                                       }
51  {                                                               }
52  {       ListOfRecords = record                                  }
53  {                    MaximumSize : 1..MaximumListSize;          }
54  {                    CurrentSize : integer;                     }
55  {                    Entries : array[1..MaximumListSize] of ListEntry }
56  {                    CurrentEntry : integer;                    }
57  {                    NextEntry : integer;                       }
58  {                  end;                                         }
59  {                                                               }
60  {  In this implementation of ListOfRecords, a list is represented by }
61  {  a record that contains the following fields:                 }
62  {                                                               }
63  {    MaximumSize - the maximum number of records in the list    }
64  {    CurrentSize - the number of records currently in the list  }
65  {    Entries - an array containing the records in the list      }
66  {    CurrentEntry - the subscript of the current record in Entries }
67  {    NextEntry - the subscript of the next record in Entries    }
68  {                                                               }
69  {  CurrentEntry is 0 if the current entry has been deleted.     }
70  {  NextEntry is 0 if the current record is the last one in the list. }
71  {  Both CurrentEntry and NextEntry are 0 if no records have yet been }
72  {  retrieved.                                                   }
73  {                                                               }
74  {  The records in the list always occupy contiguous elements of the }
75  {  array Entries.  The first record occupies the element with   }
76  {  subscript 1, and the last record occupies the element with   }
77  {  subscript CurrentSize.  When a record is deleted from the list, }
78  {  the remaining records are rearranged as needed to maintain this }
79  {  arrangement.                                                 }
80  {---------------------------------------------------------------}
81
82
83  procedure InitList (var List : ListOfRecords; ListLimit : integer);
84
85     {------------------------------------------------------------}
86     {  InitList initializes a new (empty) list, setting its maximum }
87     {  size to the value specified in ListLimit.  If the list size }
88     {  specified is too large, an error message is displayed and the }
89     {  maximum allowable list size is used.                       }
90     {                                                            }
91     {  Input parameters:                                         }
92     {    List - the list to be initialized                       }
93     {    ListLimit - the maximum size of the list                }
94     {                                                            }
95     {  Output parameters:                                        }
96     {    List - the initialized list                             }
```

```
97        {-------------------------------------------------------------------}
98
99        begin   { InitList }
100
101          if ListLimit > MaximumListSize then
102            begin
103              writeln('*** InitList: specified size is greater than maximum');
104              List.MaximumSize := MaximumListSize
105            end  { if }
106          else
107            List.MaximumSize := ListLimit;
108          List.CurrentSize := 0;
109          List.CurrentEntry := 0;
110          List.NextEntry := 0
111
112        end;   { InitList }
113
114    {++++++++++++++++++++++++++++++++++++++++++++++++++++++++++++++++++++++++}
115
116    procedure GetFirst(var List : ListOfRecords; var Entry : ListEntry;
117                       var EndOfList : boolean);
118
119        {-------------------------------------------------------------------}
120        {  GetFirst gets the first entry (if any) in List, returning it in  }
121        {  the parameter Entry.  The entry retrieved is made the current    }
122        {  entry for the list.  The following entry (if any) is made the    }
123        {  next entry.  If the list contains no entries, EndOfList is set   }
124        {  to true; otherwise, EndOfList is set to false.                   }
125        {                                                                   }
126        {  Input parameters:                                                }
127        {    List - the list whose first entry is to be retrieved           }
128        {                                                                   }
129        {  Output parameters:                                               }
130        {    List - current entry set to the entry retrieved, and next      }
131        {           entry set to the following entry (if any)               }
132        {    Entry - the first entry in List; this parameter remains        }
133        {            unchanged if the list is empty                         }
134        {    EndOfList - true if List is empty; false otherwise             }
135        {-------------------------------------------------------------------}
136
137        begin   { GetFirst }
138
139          if List.CurrentSize = 0 then
140            EndOfList := true
141          else
142            begin
143              List.CurrentEntry := 1;
144              if List.CurrentEntry = List.CurrentSize then
145                List.NextEntry := 0
146              else
147                List.NextEntry := List.CurrentEntry + 1;
148              Entry := List.Entries[List.CurrentEntry];
149              EndOfList := false
```

```
150            end  { else }
151
152      end;   { GetFirst }
153
154   {++++++++++++++++++++++++++++++++++++++++++++++++++++++++++++++++}
155
156   procedure GetNext(var List : ListOfRecords; var Entry : ListEntry;
157                     var EndOfList : boolean);
158
159      {-----------------------------------------------------------------}
160      {  GetNext gets the next entry in List (if any), returning it in  }
161      {  the parameter Entry.  If there is no next entry in the list,   }
162      {  EndOfList is set to true; otherwise, EndOfList is set to false. }
163      {                                                                 }
164      {  The entry retrieved (if any) is made the current entry for the }
165      {  list. The following entry (if any) is made the next entry.     }
166      {                                                                 }
167      {  Input parameters:                                              }
168      {     List - the list whose next entry is to be retrieved         }
169      {                                                                 }
170      {  Output parameters:                                             }
171      {     List - current entry set to the entry retrieved, and next   }
172      {            entry set to the following entry (if any)            }
173      {     Entry - the next entry in List; this parameter remains      }
174      {             unchanged if there is no next entry to retrieve     }
175      {     EndOfList - true if there was no next entry to retrieve;    }
176      {                 false otherwise                                 }
177      {-----------------------------------------------------------------}
178
179      begin  { GetNext }
180
181         if List.NextEntry = 0 then
182            EndOfList := true
183         else
184            begin
185               List.CurrentEntry := List.NextEntry;
186               if List.CurrentEntry = List.CurrentSize then
187                  List.NextEntry := 0
188               else
189                  List.NextEntry := List.CurrentEntry + 1;
190               Entry := List.Entries[List.CurrentEntry];
191               EndOfList := false
192            end
193
194      end;   { GetNext }
195
196   {++++++++++++++++++++++++++++++++++++++++++++++++++++++++++++++++}
197
198   procedure AddNew(var List : ListOfRecords; NewEntry : ListEntry);
199
200      {-----------------------------------------------------------------}
201      {  AddNew adds the entry NewEntry to List.  If the list is already }
202      {  at its maximum size, an error message is displayed and the      }
```

```
203   {  new entry is not added.  The current list entry is not changed   }
204   {  by this operation. If the next entry in the list was previously  }
205   {  undefined, the new entry becomes the next entry.                 }
206   {                                                                    }
207   {  Input parameters:                                                 }
208   {    List - the list to which NewEntry is to be added               }
209   {    NewEntry - the entry to add                                     }
210   {                                                                    }
211   {  Output parameters:                                                }
212   {    List - with NewEntry added at the end of the list              }
213   {--------------------------------------------------------------------}
214
215   begin   { AddNew }
216
217     if List.CurrentSize = List.MaximumSize then
218       writeln('*** AddNew: list overflow')
219     else
220       begin
221         List.CurrentSize := List.CurrentSize + 1;
222         List.Entries[List.CurrentSize] := NewEntry;
223         if List.NextEntry = 0 then
224           List.NextEntry := List.CurrentSize
225       end   { else }
226
227   end;   { AddNew }
228
229   {++++++++++++++++++++++++++++++++++++++++++++++++++++++++++++++++++++++}
230
231   procedure DeleteCurrent(var List : ListOfRecords);
232
233     {--------------------------------------------------------------------}
234     {  DeleteCurrent deletes the current entry from List.  If there is   }
235     {  no current entry defined, an error message is displayed. The      }
236     {  current entry for the list becomes undefined after this           }
237     {  operation.                                                        }
238     {                                                                    }
239     {  If the entry being deleted is not the last one in the list, the   }
240     {  last entry in the list is shifted to replace the entry that was   }
241     {  deleted.  (This is done to avoid leaving unused entries within    }
242     {  the list.)  This entry becomes the new next entry in the list.    }
243     {                                                                    }
244     {  Input parameters:                                                 }
245     {    List - the list whose current entry is to be deleted           }
246     {                                                                    }
247     {  Output parameters:                                                }
248     {    List - with the entry deleted                                   }
249     {--------------------------------------------------------------------}
250
251   begin   { DeleteCurrent }
252
253     if List.CurrentEntry = 0 then
254       writeln('*** DeleteCurrent: no current entry to delete')
255     else
```

```
256          begin
257             if List.CurrentEntry < List.CurrentSize then
258               begin
259                 List.Entries[List.CurrentEntry] := List.Entries[List.CurrentSize];
260                 List.NextEntry := List.CurrentEntry
261               end; { if }
262             List.CurrentSize := List.CurrentSize - 1;
263             List.CurrentEntry := 0
264          end   { else }
265
266     end;  { DeleteCurrent }
267
268  {++++++++++++++++++++++++++++++++++++++++++++++++++++++++++++++++++++++++++}
269
270  procedure UpdateCurrent(var List : ListOfRecords; Entry : ListEntry);
271
272     {----------------------------------------------------------------------}
273     { UpdateCurrent updates the current entry in List, replacing it       }
274     { with Entry.  If there is no current entry defined, an error         }
275     { message is displayed.  After this operation, the current entry      }
276     { remains the one that was updated (with the new contents).           }
277     {                                                                     }
278     { Input parameters:                                                   }
279     {   List - the list whose current entry is to be updated              }
280     {   Entry - the new contents for the current entry                    }
281     {                                                                     }
282     { Output parameters:                                                  }
283     {   List - with the current entry updated                            }
284     {----------------------------------------------------------------------}
285
286     begin   { UpdateCurrent }
287
288        if List.CurrentEntry = 0 then
289           writeln('*** UpdateCurrent: no current entry to update')
290        else
291           List.Entries[List.CurrentEntry] := Entry
292
293     end;  { UpdateCurrent }
294
295  {++++++++++++++++++++++++++++++++++++++++++++++++++++++++++++++++++++++++++}
296
297  function NumberIn(var List : ListOfRecords) : integer;
298
299     {----------------------------------------------------------------------}
300     { NumberIn returns a function value equal to the current number of    }
301     { entries in List.                                                    }
302     {                                                                     }
303     { Input parameters:                                                   }
304     {   List - the list whose number of entries is to be returned         }
305     {      Note: List is a var parameter for efficiency in parameter      }
306     {            passing.                                                 }
307     {                                                                     }
308     { Output parameters: None                                            }
```

```
309     {                                                                 }
310     {   Function value: the current number of entries in List         }
311     {-----------------------------------------------------------------}
312
313     begin   { NumberIn }
314
315       NumberIn := List.CurrentSize
316
317     end;   { NumberIn }
```

INCLUDE FILE

screen.i

```
 1    {*******************************************************************}
 2
 3    { ## Non-standard statements -- Berkeley Pascal version }
 4    {
 5    procedure ClrScr; external;
 6    }
 7    { End Berkeley Pascal version }
 8
 9    procedure ClearScreen;
10
11       {-----------------------------------------------------------------}
12       {  ClearScreen clears the terminal screen and positions the      }
13       {  cursor at the upper left corner of the screen.  It calls a    }
14       {  non-standard Pascal library routine to perform this operation. }
15       {-----------------------------------------------------------------}
16
17       begin
18         ClrScr   { call library routine ClrScr to clear screen }
19       end;  { ClearScreen }
20
21    {*******************************************************************}
22
23    { ## Non-standard statements -- Berkeley Pascal version }
24    {
25    procedure GotoXY(x,y : integer); external;
26    }
27    { End Berkeley Pascal version }
28
29    procedure MoveCursor(Row, Col : integer);
30
31       {-----------------------------------------------------------------}
32       {  MoveCursor moves the cursor on the terminal screen to the     }
33       {  row and column given by its input parameters.  The next write }
34       {  or writeln operation that sends output to the terminal will   }
35       {  begin writing at the row and column location designated.  The }
36       {  procedure calls a non-standard Pascal library routine to perform }
37       {  this operation.                                                }
38       {                                                                 }
39       {  Input parameters:                                              }
40       {    Row,Col - the row (line) and column (horizontal position) on }
41       {              the screen to which the cursor is to be moved.  The }
42       {              upper left-hand corner of the screen is row 1, column 1. }
43       {-----------------------------------------------------------------}
```

```
44
45      begin
46
47        { call library routine GotoXY to move the cursor -- note that
48           GotoXY expects the column value as its first parameter }
49
50        GotoXY(Col,Row)
51      end;   { MoveCursor }
52
53   {*******************************************************************}
54
55   { ## Non-standard statements -- Berkeley Pascal version }
56   {
57   procedure ClrEol; external;
58   }
59   { End Berkeley Pascal version }
60
61   procedure ClearLine;
62
63      {------------------------------------------------------------}
64      {   ClearLine clears the line on the terminal screen where the     }
65      {   cursor is currently positioned, from the cursor position to the }
66      {   end of the line.  It calls a non-standard Pascal library routine }
67      {   to perform this function.                                      }
68      {------------------------------------------------------------}
69
70      begin
71        ClrEol      { call library routine ClrEol to clear line }
72      end;   { ClearLine }
```

QUICK REFERENCE GUIDE TO
DOS Commands

The following are some of the most commonly used DOS commands. Many of these commands have other options that can be specified, and there are also many other commands available. If you are interested in learning more about DOS, your instructor can tell you where to find reference material.

drive :   Change the default disk to the drive specified.

cd *dir1*   Change the working directory to *dir1*.

cd \   Change the working directory to the main directory of the default disk.

copy *file1 file2*   Copy *file1* to *file2*. After the copy is executed, *file1* still exists.

copy *file1 dir1*   Copy *file1* into directory *dir1*. After the copy is executed, *file1* still exists in its original location.

dir   List the names of the files in the current working directory.

dir /p   List the names of the files in the current working directory, pausing after each screenful of output.

dir *dir1*   List the names of the files in directory *dir1*.

erase *file1*   Remove the file *file1*.

erase *.bak   Remove all of the files in the current working directory with the extension .BAK.

format *drive* :   Format a disk in the specified drive. (*Warning:* this erases any previous information on the disk -- do not use this command with the hard disk.)

`mkdir` *dir1*	Make a new directory named *dir1*.
`print` *file1*	Print the contents of *file1* on the line printer.
`rename` *file1 file2*	Change the name of *file1* to *file2*.
`turbo` *file1*	Start Turbo Pascal and open the file *file1*.
`type` *file1*	Display the contents of the file *file1* on the screen.
`type` *file1* `| more`	Display the contents of the file *file1* on the screen. After each screenful of output, pause until the user presses \<Enter\>.
`xcopy -r` *dir1 dir2*	Copy all of the files from directory *dir1* into *dir2*. After the `xcopy` is executed, all of the files still exist in their original location.

File names in most DOS commands can be specified using any of the following forms:

file-name	A file in the current working directory.
directory-name\file-name	A file in a subdirectory of the current directory.
\directory-name\file-name	A file in another directory on the default drive.
drive :*directory-name\file-name*	A file in a directory on another drive.

QUICK REFERENCE GUIDE TO

The Turbo Pascal IDE

This section summarizes some of the most useful features of the Turbo Pascal Integrated Development Environment (IDE). There are also many other commands and features available in the IDE. If you are interested in learning more, check the Turbo Pascal manuals or other reference sources suggested by your instructor.

Each entry in the following tables shows the menu selection or keys that accomplish the indicated operation. Hot key alternatives for menu selections are enclosed in [...]. These menu selections correspond to Version 7.0 of Turbo Pascal. Footnotes are used to indicate any differences for Version 6.0.

Moving the Cursor

Move one line or column at a time	↑ ↓ ← →
Move one page at a time	\<PgDn\> \<PgUp\>
Move to beginning of current line	\<Home\>
Move to end of current line	\<End\>
Search for specified text	Search | Find
Repeat the previous search	Search | Search again

Editing the Program

Insert text in the program	Type the text to be inserted	
Delete the character under the cursor	<Del>	
Highlight a block of text	<Shift> + arrow keys	
Delete a highlighted block	Edit	Clear	[Ctrl+Del]
Delete a block and save it on the clipboard	Edit	Cut	[Shift+Del]
Copy a highlighted block to the clipboard	Edit	Copy	[Ctrl+Ins]
Insert text from the clipboard	Edit	Paste	[Shift+Ins]
Search for text and replace it with new text	Search	Replace	
Undo the last editing operation (not available in Turbo Pascal 6.0)	Edit	Undo	[Alt+BkSp]

Compiling and Running

Compile the program	Compile	Compile	[Alt+F9]
Run the program	Run	Run	[Ctrl+F9]
Interrupt execution of the program	<Ctrl+Break>	
Set compiler options (error checking, etc.)	Options	Compiler	

Debugging

Execute the next instruction (procedure calls treated as one instruction)	Run I Step over	[F8]
Execute the next instruction (tracing into called procedures)	Run I Trace into	[F7]
View the full output screen (temporarily)	Debug I User screen[1]	[Alt+F5]
View the output screen (in a new window)	Debug I Output[1]	
Watch the value of a variable or expression	Debug I Add watch[2]	[Ctrl+F7]
Run and stop at the cursor position	Run I Go to cursor	[F4]
Stop execution at a specified point	Debug I Add breakpoint[3]	
Start over from the beginning of the program	Run I Program reset	[Ctrl+F2]

---

[1]In Turbo Pascal 6.0, these choices are under the Window menu
[2]In Turbo Pascal 6.0, use Debug I Watches I Add watch
[3]In Turbo Pascal 6.0, use Debug I Breakpoints

Managing Windows

Open a file in a new window	File	Open	[F3]
Activate the next window in sequence	Window	Next	[F6]
Close the active window	Window	Close	[Alt+F3]
Rearrange open windows to fit on the screen	Window	Tile	
Resize or move the active window	Window	Size/Move [Ctrl+F5]	

Saving and Printing Files

Save the file in the active window on disk	File	Save	[F2]
Print the contents of the active window	File	Print	
Exit Turbo Pascal	File	Exit	[Alt+X]

Getting Help

Ask for help on the operation being performed (can be used at any time)	<F1>
Table of contents for the online Help system	Help	Contents
Help on using the Help system	Help	Using help

 **APPENDIX**

Using this Book for Independent Study

The instructions in this lab manual assume that your instructor has already set up the example programs on your computer. If you are using *Pascal: A Guided Tour* to learn Pascal on your own (instead of as part of a class), you will need to do this yourself. There are also a few other minor differences in the procedures you will follow as you do the exercises.

Getting the Example Programs

The example programs for use with this manual are available via Internet by anonymous `ftp`. (If you are not already familiar with `ftp`, a good reference book is *A Student's Guide to UNIX,* by Harley Hahn.) Use the following procedure to get the programs:

1. Connect to `ucssun1.sdsu.edu`
2. Login as `anonymous`
3. Change directory to `faculty/beck`
4. Get the `README` file, which contains further instructions.

The procedure described in the `README` file will copy all of the example programs to a directory named `\PROGRAMS` on your hard disk. The programs are stored in several subdirectories. After you have installed the programs, the contents of `\PROGRAMS` should look like

```
CHAP1      <DIR>      3-09-94    1:02p
CHAP2      <DIR>      3-09-94    1:02p
CHAP3      <DIR>      3-09-94    1:02p
CHAP4      <DIR>      3-09-94    1:02p
CHAP5      <DIR>      3-09-94    1:03p
CHAP6      <DIR>      3-09-94    1:03p
CHAP7      <DIR>      3-09-94    1:03p
CHAP8      <DIR>      3-09-94    1:03p
CHAP9      <DIR>      3-09-94    1:04p
CHAP10     <DIR>      3-09-94    1:04p
CHAP11     <DIR>      3-09-94    1:04p
```

```
CHAP12      <DIR>          3-09-94    1:06p
CHAP13      <DIR>          3-09-94    1:06p
CHAP14      <DIR>          3-09-94    1:06p
DICTION     <DIR>          3-09-94    1:06p
```

You may also want to make a backup copy of the example programs in a different directory or on a different disk.

Running from the Hard Disk

If you are using this book for independent study, you are probably using your own PC. In that case, you will find it most convenient to run the exercises directly from the hard disk, instead of copying the programs to floppy disks. At the beginning of each chapter, simply change to the directory that contains the programs for that chapter. For example, at the beginning of Chapter 1 enter the command

```
cd \programs\chap1
```

instead of the commands

```
a:
cd \
```

that are described in this manual. Your DOS prompt will reflect this change -- for example, in Chapter 1 the prompt should look like `C:\PROGRAMS\CHAP1>` instead of `A:>`.

INDEX